PROBLEMS OF
MODERN
GOVERNMENT
A NORTON SERIES

Public policies and their politics

An introduction to the techniques
of government control

Edited by

RANDALL B. RIPLEY

PROBLEMS OF MODERN GOVERNMENT

Public Policies and Their Politics

PROBLEMS OF MODERN GOVERNMENT

General Editor: **THEODORE J.** LOWI, *University of Chicago*

Each volume in this series examines
questions of public policy within their
political context

PRIVATE LIFE AND PUBLIC ORDER

PUBLIC POLICIES AND THEIR POLITICS

THE POLITICS OF EDUCATION

Public Policies and Their Politics

TECHNIQUES OF GOVERNMENT CONTROL

Edited with an introduction by
RANDALL B. RIPLEY
THE BROOKINGS INSTITUTION

NEW YORK
W · W · NORTON & COMPANY · INC ·

"Social Techniques" from: Robert A. Dahl and Charles E. Lindblom, *Politics, Economics and Welfare*, pp. 6–17. Copyright, 1953, by Harper & Brothers. Reprinted by permission of Harper & Row, Publisher.

"The Scope and Bias of the Pressure System" from: E. E. Schattschneider, *The Semisovereign People*. Copyright © 1960 by E. E. Schattschneider. Reprinted by permission of the author and publisher, Holt, Rinehart and Winston, Inc. *All rights reserved*.

"Distribution, Regulation, Redistribution: The Functions of Government" from: Theodore J. Lowi, "American Business, Public Policy, Case-Studies and Political Theory," *World Politics*, Vol. XVI, No. 4, July 1964.

"How Special Tax Provisions Get Enacted" from: Stanley S. Surrey, "The Congress and the Tax Lobbyist—How Special Tax Provisions Get Enacted," 70 *Harvard Law Review* 1145 (1957). Copyright © 1957 by The Harvard Law Review Association.

"The Patent System in Action" from: Walton Hamilton, *The Politics of Industry*. Copyright 1957 by the Regents of the University of Michigan. Reprinted by permission of Alfred A. Knopf, Inc.

"The Political Impasse in Farm Support Legislation," *Yale Law Journal*, April 1962, pp. 952–967, 969–70. Copyright by the Yale Law Journal Company. Reprinted by permission.

"Antitrust is Pro-Business" by Lee Loevinger from the August 1962 issue of *Fortune* Magazine by special permission; © 1962 Time, Inc.

"The Crisis in Antitrust" by Robert H. Bork and Ward S. Bowman, Jr. from the August 1962 issue of *Fortune* Magazine by special permission; © 1962 Time, Inc.

"The Root of the FTC's Confusion" by Harold B. Meyers from the August 1963 issue of *Fortune* Magazine by special permission; © 1963 Time, Inc.

"The Steel-price Controversy 1962" from: Grant McConnell, *Steel and the Presidency*. Reprinted by permission of W. W. Norton & Company, Inc. Copyright © 1963 by W. W. Norton & Company, Inc.

"The Budget and Economic Growth" from *The Budget and Economic Growth*, Committee for Economic Development, New York, 1959, pp. 8–19.

"Revenue and Redistribution of Wealth" from: John Morton Blum, *From the Morgenthau Diaries: Years of Crisis, 1928–1938*, 1959. Reprinted by permission of Houghton Mifflin Company.

"Taxation and Monopoly Power" from: Fritz Machlup, *The Political Economy of Monopoly*, 1952. Reprinted by permission of the Johns Hopkins Press.

I am grateful to Professor Theodore J. Lowi of the University of Chicago and general editor for the series in which this volume is included, to Professor Leslie Gelb and Professor Nelson Polsby of Wesleyan University, and to my wife, Vivian, for the interest in and comments on this enterprise. R.B.R.

Contents

23790

Introduction: The Politics of Public Policy

SPECIFIC DECISIONS about public policy set the bounds within which the government must operate. They also give some degree of direct instruction as to how it should operate. All public policy decisions reflect the ends of governmental activity. Taken singly and together, they determine the extent to which a government is committed to programs that promote the general welfare. An understanding of the making of public policy decisions is essential for anyone who cares about the goals which the nation sets for itself.

Observers of the American political process can view the activity of the federal government in domestic economic and social matters through several lenses. They can focus on the source and amount of government funds for given purposes. They can look at the impact of the government's activity on society, including questions of quantity and quality: who benefits how much at the expense of whom. Or they can look primarily at the instruments or methods which the government uses in implementing its programs—the techniques of government control.

THE ORIGINS OF GOVERNMENT CONTROL

The attainment of economic and social justice has been the growing concern of the American government since its establishment. Political leaders of the eighteenth and early nineteenth centuries saw problems involving equality and inequality, privilege and deprivation, wealth and poverty. But they were timid —by our standards—in linking the Federal Government to any but the most peripheral attacks on these problems. The broad solution adopted in the first seventy-five years of the Republic was to expand the field of opportunity for all Americans by selective governmental actions. Thus the controversies over the Louisiana Purchase, Texas, Oregon, "manifest destiny," internal improvements, railroad building, homesteads, and the tariff were all posing the same choice: should the government help expand the opportunity for individual (and, increasingly, corporate)

Americans to succeed economically or should it do nothing? The country almost always opted in favor of government activity. *Subsidy* was thus accepted as a legitimate endeavor for the central government to undertake.

Once the Civil War had demonstrated that the Federal Government was also a national government, new problems began to arise that involved public discussion of what the government should do. Corporate wealth, which rapidly made the Republican Party its political handmaiden, began to alter the dimensions of American opportunity. The end of the homesteading era and the massive waves of immigration from Eastern and Southern Europe compounded the new problems.

The political system took about twenty years to frame even the beginnings of a coherent response. The response came in the form of adding *regulation* to the legitimate sphere of government activity. Thus slowly, unsurely, and hesitatingly the government began to tell the owners of railroads and the formers of trusts that they could not behave in certain ways. Members of the Republican Party formerly subservient to business interests were willing to deliver this message to their erstwhile friends. In the late nineteenth century Congress began the long development of railroad regulation and antitrust activity with passage of the Interstate Commerce Act in 1887 and the Sherman Antitrust Act in 1890. In the first fifteen years of the twentieth century new laws pursued the same ends. Several laws in the first decade of the new century made railroad regulation tighter. The first two years of Woodrow Wilson's presidency (1913 and 1914) saw the passage of the Clayton Act and the Federal Trade Commission Act, both aimed at the trusts and at restraint of trade in general. Related major laws such as the Underwood-Simmons Tariff and the Federal Reserve Act were also designed to make American business pursue profit honestly.

It took the catastrophe of an economic depression seemingly irreversible by normal means to legitimize the activity of *manipulation* on the part of the Federal government. The economic disaster of the 1930s revealed the corresponding social disaster that had been developing for a number of decades. The government was given authority to relieve both economic and social deprivation and to prevent the recurrence of at least the most visible parts of both of them. Now the government could, with the approval of a majority of the nation's citizens, attempt to change the environment of those citizens so that the gulf between the indulged and deprived might shrink.

It took yet another crisis—the involvement of over 10 million men directly (and the entire nation indirectly) in World War II —to expand even further the sphere of manipulative government action. To the government was given responsibility for control of prices, wages, rents, and profits. Eventually, the social upheavals caused by the war made race the province of substantial government activity.

Thus, by the mid-1960s governmental techniques of influencing what goes on in the private sphere and, in a sense, mingling the public and private orders, could legitimately be aimed at three things: the rate of private activity (where techniques of subsidy could be used), the conditions under which private activity can take place (where techniques of regulation could be used), and the rewards for private activity (where techniques of manipulation could be used).

A BRIEF CATALOG OF TECHNIQUES

Techniques for subsidizing are aimed at increasing the rates of private activity in certain defined fields and, usually, at increasing the rewards for such activity simultaneously. By tradition, the tariff and the patent have both been used as subsidies. More recently, subsidies have been given through grants-in-aid, grants of special privilege, and aid to public works. Two of the newest fields receiving massive subsidy are science and education.

The techniques which the Federal Government has been able to develop and use in the interests of subsidy are numerous. A few of the more important ones in the 1960s include research grants, grants-in-aid, price support, procurement of materials, and taxation. Research grants are currently especially important in the space field and in scientific development in general. Grants-in-aid are used to subsidize activity in the fields of education, mental health, hospital construction, and airport construction, among others. Price supports have provided billions of dollars of subsidy to the American farmer. Many more billions are spent on procuring the equipment which the government needs. The magnitude of expenditure is especially large in the building of a vast military arsenal to meet the varied demands of modern defense. Taxes can be used to subsidize by granting exemptions and special tax rates to certain types of persons, corporations, or activities.

Techniques for regulating are aimed at prescribing specific conditions under which private activity can and cannot take place. Regulatory techniques seek to limit the alternatives open to private parties. The traditional Federal concern for regulation was centered in the transportation field and in the field of anti-trust activity. More recent additions to the list of regulated fields include labor relations, power, broadcasting, and the securities market. By the mid-1960s the Federal Government had developed and used a wide range of regulatory techniques in almost every segment of the American economy and society. At the same time, some of the traditional regulatory agencies and techniques were being transformed into the captives of those who were supposed to be regulated.

Specific regulatory techniques are numerous. Some of the more important ones at the present time include dissolution of private arrangements, pricing prohibitions, judicial and quasi-judicial proceedings, public appeals (especially by the President), certificates of convenience, necessity, or safety, and taxation.

The government has been interested in dissolving private arrangements that run counter to the public interest since the Sherman Act of 1890. Since then the number and variety of prohibited arrangements have multiplied. Certain kinds of price policies are prohibited and others are limited under various statutes. The government can go to court to request abatement of certain practices—air and water pollution of a specific description, for example. The regulatory commissions themselves act in part like courts and thus a cease-and-desist order from the Federal Trade Commission comes only after a hearing in which the parties accused of unlawful business practices participate. Public appeals by the President have a regulatory impact. If a President asks for stable prices or stable wages in certain industries, his words, particularly if backed by a willingness to use the prestige and power of his office, are an attempt to prescribe conditions under which private activity can take place.

Many government agencies issue certificates allowing certain kinds of activity to proceed because given conditions have been met. The Federal Aviation Agency, for example, certifies airplanes to be safe before they can fly on commercial routes. Taxation can also be used to regulate private activity. High taxes on certain kinds of goods deemed to be socially harmful can in effect keep their production low or eliminate it altogether.

Techniques for manipulating aim to alter the reward structure for certain activities in favor of some citizens or groups of citizens at the expense of other citizens or groups of citizens. These techniques change the environment so that the economic, social, or political shares received by identifiable sectors or groups are changed. These techniques inevitably enrich some (economically, socially, or politically) at the expense of others. Taxation is the traditional manipulative technique used by the federal government. In recent years new fiscal and monetary techniques for reducing social imbalance and inequality have been developed. The fiscal agencies of the government operate using their powers over interest rates, discount rates, and bank reserve requirements for redistributive ends. Insurance schemes—such as Social Security and Medicare—have definite manipulative ends. Legislation which may appear to be regulatory—such as wages and hours laws—may actually be used for manipulative ends. In the labor and civil rights fields the government has developed a whole range of new manipulative techniques—including the mediation of labor disputes and numerous ways of using the government's persuasive and financial powers in the cause of equal rights for all citizens.

In short, the government has through the years developed a wide variety and range of techniques which it can use for developing the kind of control which it desires. Techniques aimed at subsidizing certain individuals or groups of individuals are selective in impact—with the whole society unaware of the use of the technique. The permissive nature of techniques of subsidy also keeps their visibility low except to those directly affected. Most important in keeping these techniques partially unseen in society is the distance which they maintain between those who benefit from them and those who do not. No one perceives that he is directly suffering because the government is subsidizing someone else. An individual cannot calculate that he is losing merely because someone else is gaining.

Techniques designed to regulate certain individuals or groups are also selective in impact. But they are used in connection with restriction and thus the level of political visibility begins to rise. Furthermore, the regulated and the unregulated can compare what each has gained or lost. Or, if the technique of regulation requires choosing between two individuals, companies, or groups and regulating in favor of the interest of one and in opposition to the interest of the other, political visibility is certainly going to be high.

Techniques aimed at manipulating the political and social environment (usually in the interests of equality—or inequality) are the most visible. They are collective or social in impact. Large chunks of the population are affected in the same way and are made aware of the impact of the technique at about the same time. For example, millions of Americans would know almost immediately about and have direct experience of the impact of any change of income tax rates or, to a lesser degree, the minimum wage rate. The restrictive character of the technique may be blurred since its impact is on the environment and not on the individual. But the computation of losses and gains is quickly made public by the more articulate representatives of those affected—both those who consider themselves to be benefited by the use of the technique and those who consider themselves the victims. Thus, in using techniques aimed at manipulating the environment, the government is involving itself heavily in basic social and economic divisions in the polity. The general thrust of governmental manipulative activity has been to lessen the deprivation of the underprivileged.

Taken together, all three types of technique provide the basis for a more precise assessment of the direction in which the government is heading in any given period of time. Manipulative techniques may benefit the deprived when at the same time regulative or subsidizing techniques are used to extend additional favors to the already privileged. At other times all techniques may be aimed at helping the underprivileged. At still other times all techniques may be used to convey further benefits to the already overprivileged. Breaking governmental action into segments by technique permits a more sophisticated appraisal of the government's over-all social and economic intentions.

THE CHARACTER OF TECHNIQUES

The readings in this volume indicate some of the ways in which political actors perceive techniques of government control and how they attempt to use these techniques to gain specific objectives. It is in the regulative field, for example, that techniques themselves become the object of primary political interest and discussion. Thus the exact hearing procedures used by the Federal Communications Commission or the Federal Trade Commission are the subject of much earnest discussion by those affected. In the field of subsidy the central political consideration is the question of how much goes to whom. When the government decides to give certain types of aid to education, for example, the primary concern at the outset is in devising the precise formula for apportioning the aid to different states and localities. When manipulative techniques are used, the political participants are most likely to ask either about the source and size of the governmental funds involved or about who benefits *at the expense of whom*. Changes in tax rates prompt questions of this character. In instances of subsidy and manipulation, then, the techniques are usually viewed indirectly. Other questions are asked first in most cases.

The following simple chart illustrates where the most heightened political perception is likely to occur. The asterisks represent the focus of primary political attention.

Central Political Consideration	*Purpose of Technique*		
	Subsidy	*Regulation*	*Manipulation*
Source and size of government funds			✼✼✼
Government control		✼✼✼	
Impact of government program (amount)	✼✼✼		
Impact of government program (amount; at expense of whom?)			✼✼✼

In general, four points about the complexities of studying techniques of control should be made. First, in common political parlance techniques are often misunderstood and mislabeled—sometimes willfully. For example, as Dahl and Lindblom point out, "socialized medicine," considered in one way, is far more private in nature than is the contracting out of government business to "free enterprise." [1]

Second, a single government program can contain a bundle of

1. For Dahl and Lindblom's discussion of "social techniques" see pp. 1–13 of this volume.

different techniques. The program of the Tennessee Valley Authority is a good example of this complexity. So is the Social Security system, which embraces not only social insurance but also special public assistance, special veterans' security measures, general assistance,[2] and Medicare.

Third, some techniques which are important to the government are not usually thought of as techniques of control at all. For example, research and the expenditure of research money can be an important technique. Likewise, the conscious choice of unrestricted business enterprise is a technique. Even sophisticated thinkers tend to assume laissez-faire as a starting point. But, by the mid-twentieth century, it clearly is no longer the automatic starting point. Indeed, a governmental decision to forego control in a specific situation may be more conscious and pointed and controversial than the choice of almost any other alternative.

Fourth, all of the various techniques can be studied by looking at the related political process at any one (or combination) of a number of points. To simplify, a technique can be studied through the filters of congressional politics, electoral politics, group politics, bureaucratic politics, judicial politics, and the politics of federalism.

In the policy process the choice of techniques is crucial. This choice helps shape both the political configuration surrounding either a legislative or an administrative battle and it also helps shape the impact of the policy involved. What can be learned from a study of techniques? To put the question another way: what of political significance can be predicted from a study of techniques of government control?

First, those advocating either the use of techniques by the government or legislation providing the government with new techniques will choose those techniques which best serve their real ends. For example, if some kind of legislation regulating guns seems inevitable then those wanting little difficulty placed between a buyer and a gun will opt for a reporting or informational technique as the strongest which the government should have. Those desiring severely restricted distribution of guns will opt for a technique involving prohibition and criminal penalties.

2. These first four rubrics are taken from Eveline Burns, *The American Social Security System* (Boston: Houghton Mifflin, 1949), pp. 46–52.

Second, different techniques tend to involve different participants—regardless of whether the technique is aimed at subsidy, regulation, or manipulation. Research contracts and procurement as techniques promoting subsidy involve a large continuing role for Congress. Some techniques promoting subsidy involve a large continuing role for interest groups.

Third, some techniques are more likely than others to involve partisan political debate. Antitrust activity brings party politics into play. Farm subsidies can involve a high degree of partisan debate. A general manipulative measure involving standards like minimum wage and maximum hours laws will evoke much partisan conflict.

On the other hand, some issues do not generate partisan debate. Patents and the closing of tax loopholes are good examples. The presence or lack of partisan debate is related to the degree of visibility, which is in part the result of the technique chosen. Patents are likely never to become highly visible even to a politically articulate public. A broad-scale minimum wage law affecting large portions of the society is automatically highly visible.

Fourth, some techniques are more susceptible to capture by non-governmental forces than others and some are more likely to include exemptions than others. Taxes are certainly subject to demands for exemptions. General wage and hour standards are often amended to exempt certain classes of workers. One technique which seems to have been captured by private forces is the issuing of grazing permits. The Interstate Commerce Commission is thought by many to have become the spokesman for the railroads.

Fifth, a close study of techniques reveals the changing purpose of certain public policies. For example, grazing permits intended to subsidize a broad range of livestock raisers was limited to a narrow range by the activities of private forces. Thus the policy was used to manipulate a specific environment for the benefit of a few—and the original subsidizing intent was subverted.

One word of warning is necessary: obviously a study of techniques cannot tell us everything about a political situation. One must also know about the specific institutions involved in a given political fight, the individual persons involved, and the broader political context surrounding the fight. But a study of techniques is a profitable place to begin the task of understanding the relations between politics, policies, and the government.

THE PARTICIPANTS AND THE POLICIES

The readings in Part One present three different ways of looking at the role of the political actors in determining public policy. Dahl and Lindblom discuss "social techniques" and indicate the relation between them and "private enterprise" and "public enterprise." In their view the general public understanding of this relation distorts reality.

Schattschneider tries to place the role of pressure groups in the making of public decisions in proper perspective. The typical estimate of group strength is misleading in two ways: groups are seen to be more important than they really are in the sense that they are thought to have influence on virtually all governmental decisions; and "the scope and bias of the pressure system" in favor of middle-class, business-oriented groups is not accurately depicted.

Lowi, in the excerpt from his review article including a major theoretical effort of his own, categorizes domestic economic and social policies on the basis of social impact. He describes three "arenas of power," each of which "tends to develop its own characteristic political structure, political process, elites, and group relations." The three arenas are labeled distribution, regulation, and redistribution. Once a policy decision has been placed in one of the three categories then Lowi feels that certain political results can be predicted. He offers broad guidelines for placing policies in one arena or another. His comments on the place of groups should be compared with Schattschneider's.

TECHNIQUES OF SUBSIDY

Part Two is devoted to the techniques of subsidy. Leon Keyserling, who was on the "inside" of the government's economic planning for the postwar period, pleads for the use of "all of the tools in our American kit" (that is, techniques) to subsidize full employment after the end of the war. This selection illustrates how a major governmental undertaking—the Employment Act of 1946—involves a broad selection of specific techniques.

Stanley Surrey, now a Treasury Department official, discusses the factors that lead to the creation of tax "loopholes" and similar exceptions to revenue laws. These exceptions, in effect, subsidize certain kinds of persons (individual and corporate) and activities.

The economist Walton Hamilton presents three short case studies, all of which show vividly how patents as techniques of subsidy can be and are used to promote monopoly.

The editors of the *Yale Law Journal,* drawing heavily on the research of political scientist Robert Salisbury, illustrate how the long public debate over farm support legislation is centrally a debate over techniques. This debate, conducted in partisan terms, has prevented the adoption of any clear policy.

TECHNIQUES OF REGULATION

The selections in Part Three focus on techniques of regulation. Lee Loevinger, responsible for several years for the antitrust program of the Justice Department, argues that antitrust activity is really for the good of the businessman. He explains the flexibility which the Justice Department has in choosing and using specific techniques. His description of one specific technique— "release letters"—is particularly interesting.

Professors Bork and Bowman of the Yale Law School disagree with Loevinger. They feel that the general antitrust policy of the government has been permeated by an anticompetitive bias. They lay the blame for the faulty reasoning surrounding the techniques of antitrust on all of the major governmental participants: the Supreme Court, the enforcement agencies, and Congress.

Harold Meyers argues that one of the enforcement agencies responsible for a different part of the general antitrust effort than the Justice Department—the Federal Trade Commission—possesses vast powers and numerous techniques but has never been able to develop clear policies. Therefore its decisions about the use of their techniques depend largely on personal whim.

A chairman of the Federal Reserve Board for a number of years, Marriner Eccles, discusses the wide variety of techniques which the government could use in World War II to control prices, profits, wages, and purchasing power. He urged President Roosevelt to use specific fiscal and price control techniques to prevent a runaway inflation during the war.

In 1957 a House Subcommittee asked the Civil Aeronautics Board for some specific answers about its operations. Although it took three years to answer and couched its replies in typically bureaucratic language, a section of the Committee document which resulted illustrates the pressures which can lead a regulator and the supposedly regulated to become one in purpose.

TECHNIQUES OF MANIPULATION

In Part Four the readings present some of the complexities surrounding the use of manipulative techniques. Professor McConnell discusses the public reaction to the use by the President of one specific technique—a public appeal to force the major steel companies to rescind a price increase. Many thought the President had used numerous other techniques—some of them improper—but McConnell argues that the final power which brought the steel producers to their knees was that of the market.

The Committee for Economic Development has long been concerned about the problem of how to use the federal budget to promote economic growth. At the height of the Eisenhower drive to cut the budget (1959) the Research and Policy Committee of the CED issued a statement analyzing the relations between federal spending and the inherently manipulative goal of full employment and maximum non-inflationary growth. Spending, as well as taxing, can be used to manipulate.

Fortunately for history, Franklin Roosevelt's Secretary of the Treasury, Henry Morgenthau, kept diaries. A selection from a volume by John Morton Blum based on those diaries shows that the Treasury in the early New Deal days hoped to structure taxes so as to redistribute wealth in favor of the poor. Morgenthau and others in the Administration consciously planned to use a variety of tax techniques to accomplish specific manipulative ends.

A professor of economics, Fritz Machlup, indicates that some of Morgenthau's hopes were in vain. For example, Morgenthau wanted a tax on intercorporate income in order to help keep businesses small. Twenty years later Machlup was able to conclude that this tax had accomplished almost nothing. Furthermore, the total impact of the corporate tax structure seemed to Machlup to be favorable to big business and weighted against small business.

PART ONE

The Analysis
of Public Policies

Social Techniques

ROBERT A. DAHL AND CHARLES E. LINDBLOM

*Robert A. Dahl is Sterling Professor of Political Science at Yale
University. Charles E. Lindblom is Professor of Economics at Yale
University. This article is taken from their* Politics, Economics and
Welfare *published in 1953.*

IN ECONOMIC LIFE the possibilities for rational social action, for
planning, for reform—in short, for solving problems—depend not
upon our choice among mythical grand alternatives but largely
upon choice among particular social techniques.

THE VARIETY OF TECHNIQUES

The number of alternative politico-economic techniques is tre-
mendously large. For example, the alternative forms of business
enterprise are numerous. One is called private enterprise, but its
alternative forms in turn are many. Proprietorship, partnership,
and corporation are terms suggesting three kinds of alternative
structures significantly different one from the others. Corporations
may be relatively simple structures for family ownership or complex bureaucracies with or without owner control. And a corporation under a minimum of regulation is different from one subject
to securities and exchange regulation; different again from one
embedded in a matrix of regulations developed through collective
bargaining, from one operating under the ever present threat of
antitrust action, or from one subject to rate regulation. The Fil-
bert Corporation, the Ford Motor Company, American Telephone
and Telegraph, General Motors, Hart-Schaffner-Marx, Kenne-

cott Copper, and the Pennsylvania Railroad are all corporations; but as techniques for the organization of production they differ from one another in ways quite significant for policy. Whatever the problem, whatever the goal, the number of significantly different alternative techniques will ordinarily be great.

INNOVATION IN POLITICO-ECONOMIC TECHNIQUES

Moreover, the number of alternative techniques is constantly growing by discovery, invention, and innovation. To return to the example of alternative forms of private enterprise, in the United States the Atomic Energy Commission has developed a rather distinctively new form of enterprise, although one similar to the organization of business through contracts in war. Through their contractual relations with the commission, Union Carbon and Carbide, Tennessee Eastman, General Electric, and other companies are operating under a different structure of cues and incentives from those of the other corporate forms mentioned above. Profit, in the ordinary sense of the term, is gone. So also is independence of investment decisions; price and production policies are subject to negotiation. Yet much of the initiative remains in the hands of the corporations, and their autonomy in a wide variety of decisions is relatively unaffected.

Many people think of invention and innovation in technology, but not in social structure; the bias probably accounts for a frequent failure to take account of the increasing possibilities for rational social reform through the improvement of techniques. We need only list a few inventions and discoveries to observe how they have increased the possibilities of rational social action, even if they often bring new problems in their wakes. The corporation itself was once an innovation; so also were unemployment compensation, food stamps, cost accounting, zoning, Lend-Lease, cooperatives, scientific management, points rationing, slum clearance, government old-age pensions, disability benefits, collective bargaining. Their origins are not so far distant that we cannot visualize a kind of accumulation of competence. Today, the European Payments Union and the Schuman Plan attest the inventiveness of our times.

RATE OF INNOVATION

The rate of increase in techniques is now extremely rapid. Why this is so must be a matter of speculation until the process of invention of social techniques is systematically studied. One hypothesis is that the growth of democracy has made it possible for masses of people to insist that problems be attacked where earlier the absence of any obvious solution to a problem was sufficient to deter any sustained efforts to solve it. Then, too, not until power is made democratic are the frustrations of masses of people necessarily the problems of public policy. Either way, the incentive to think constructively in terms of techniques is now much heightened. Another hypothesis, a corollary of what we have said, is that reform is turning to techniques instead of grand alternatives. A third hypothesis is that in the last few years war and defense have immensely stimulated the search for social as well as technological devices for social control, as is illustrated by the work of the RAND Corporation. [Financed by the U.S. Air Force, the RAND Corporation is a major center for social science research. *Editor*.]

A fourth hypothesis is that the discovery and invention of new social techniques are largely the product of the social sciences, which are themselves relatively new. The particular role of psychology has recently been conspicuous in providing social scientists with a wealth of ideas on how men may be influenced. Lastly, literacy, popular education, and technological revolutions in communication have provided a groundwork for many new patterns of cues and incentives. There are no doubt still other explanations to be found in great shifts in culture such as the decline of traditionalism in Western society.

The process of innovation is both scientific and political. It is not enough that new social techniques be discovered; they must also be put into use. Invention and discovery are only the beginning of a process the next step in which is innovation, a matter of politics. What we are suggesting is that this process taken as a whole is proceeding with astonishing rapidity—it is perhaps the greatest political revolution of our times. Anyone who is not impressed with it can hardly gauge the richness—and dangers— of possible social reform and, failing that, he cannot deal competently with public policy.

Rational and responsible reform may consequently suffer from a serious limitation at the hands of those who fail to grasp the fact that alternatives are many, that new ones can be expected to appear, and that they can be created. A great deal of policy analysis and formulation still rests with those to whom man is man and institutions are institutions and who think of policy as a reshuffling of the same old variables. One of Franklin Roosevelt's great skills as a political leader was his encouragement of new techniques, as illustrated by the National Recovery Administration, the National Labor Relations Board, Lend-Lease, food stamps, and the fifty-destroyer transaction. A contrast was the futile debate during the Second World War over the union shop in American industry, a debate in which many groups refused to consider any new alternatives to the open shop, closed shop, and union shop, although in the War Labor Board the debate finally came to an end with the innovation of the maintenance-of-membership technique. Similarly, one finds in the British debate over broadcasting policy a preoccupation with the British system and American commercial radio as the only two major alternatives; all too seldom attention is given to other alternatives yet to be tried and to still others unknown, yet to be invented. An old saw says that armies are always well prepared to fight the last war. Much of the discussion of social policy suffers from the same disability.

SELECTIVITY IN POLITICO-ECONOMIC TECHNIQUES

The alternative techniques available for a particular problem commonly offer a high degree of selectivity. They permit more precision in choice, more careful adaptation of means to ends, than men sometimes take account of. Consider, for example, the fine gradations in choice of alternative schemes of private enterprise permitted by its multiplicity of forms, existing and conceivable. The refinements in choice permitted by gradations in techniques are not limited to trivial differences among them. They range over a number of continua in which the opposite poles pose such critical alternatives as government power and private power, voluntarism and compulsion, centralization and decentralization, prescription and indoctrination, local determination and national determination.

We can illustrate the array of choices commonly available to policy, each one slightly different from another related to it, and at the same time emphasize once more the large numbers of alternative techniques by diagraming a number of these continua in which the variables are significant and upon which particular techniques suited to some particular problem or goal can be placed. Imagine, for example, the choices open between private ownership and public ownership as polar methods of enterprise organization. Opinions will differ, of course, as to the exact placement of some techniques on such a scale; but despite these differences, the pattern of such a continuum is as in Diagram 1.

The diagram proves nothing; it is only illustrative. Diagram 1 displays something of the variety of techniques possible between an unregulated private enterprise, on the one hand, and a business like the post office run as an ordinary government department, on the other hand. Both to illustrate how "public" ownership and "private" ownership have been stretched in meaning to cover techniques ranging over a long continuum and to show again the invalidity of thinking in terms of comprehensive systems, we have placed the techniques ordinarily associated in the public mind with private enterprise above the line and those commonly associated with socialism below. They overlap; the one set of techniques is not huddled toward one end of the scale, the second set toward the other. Note in particular the placement of "socialized" medicine.

This diagram reveals the foolishness of the debate on nationalization versus private enterprise. It suggests that the Atomic Energy Commission's contractual system may provide more comprehensive public control over enterprises than can be had through the degree of autonomy granted corporations like the nationalized enterprises of Britain or the Port of New York Authority. But whether that is true or not—and we emphasize again that the placement of techniques on such a scale as this must be arbitrary to a degree—for the particular goals sought, the AEC contractual system, like public utility regulation, worker control schemes, subsidies, or securities and exchange regulation, is often better than the formula of nationalization. But each of these techniques offers a slightly different combination of government and private control, and it is therefore possible to choose that particular combination best suited to remedy a particular organizational deficiency.

Private

DIAGRAM 1. A continuum showing some of the choices available between government ownership and private enterprise

Continuum position	Above the line (private techniques)	Below the line (government techniques)
Government	AEC lease and contract; Some types of defense contracts	An enterprise operated as an ordinary govt. dept, such as the post office
Govt. ownership of part of an industry	Regulated public utilities	Public corp. subject to ordinary govt. ministerial control — BBC, British RR, TVA, Port of London, Port of N.Y.
Joint govt.-private firm	Anti-trust; Worker control, Guilds, Syndicates	Public corp. with tripartite control — French electricity, French RR
	Subsidized corporation (regulated like those at right)	Govt. contracts with private producers, as in public housing
	Corporation subject to misc. corp. regulation, incl. labor and securities	
	Corporation subject to corporate regulation	Govt. purchases from private sellers, as in British health program and "socialized" medicine
	A hypothetical small proprietorship subject only to common law	

Below the line: techniques popularly described with words such as "government owned," and "public enterprise."

Above the line: techniques popularly described with words such as "private enterprise," private property, and "free enterprise."

On the line: techniques popularly thought to be neither clearly public nor private.

Note also that choice can range over even more precise gradations than those shown on the diagram, for many of these alternative techniques offer methods of combining public and private power with respect to any one specific kind of entrepreneurial decision which policy might wish to affect. We have also understated the possibilities of precision in choice because readability requires simplification: in most cases we have placed *types* of enterprise on the scale rather than identifying a particular enterprise. There will actually be found a gradation of choice within the type itself.

Diagram 2 illustrates a quite different kind of choice but again displays the fine gradations open to policy makers. In this diagram are arrayed at one extreme various techniques which combine information and education as techniques of control, with compulsive techniques at the other. The diagram illustrates choices among devices for settling labor disputes, which issue is, of course, only one of many possible illustrations.

The separation of techniques above and below the line is more arbitrary than in the previous diagram; we have tried to separate techniques widely considered to be persuasive (above the line) from those widely considered to be coercive (below the line). The overlap will show the invalidity of the distinction as it is often drawn, because some of the techniques widely thought to be persuasive are quite coercive; and it emphasizes again the range of variations to be found within each of the two types of techniques: information and compulsion.

The exact placement of a number of techniques may be disputed; it is a matter of subjective judgment rather than demonstrable fact. But, to repeat, we are trying to prove nothing except the fact of fine gradations in choice, and a change in rank of a number of techniques will not affect the usefulness of the diagram as an illustration. Few people will dispute the general arrangement of the techniques. A Presidential back-to-work appeal, which appears above the line on the extreme left, can be almost as compulsive as an injunction, even if the appeal is coupled with no threat at all. And although compulsory arbitration may be quite compulsive where awards can be enforced, it can also be no more so than a fact-finding board without power to issue a decision. Compulsory arbitration often lacks an effective penalty for disobedience; we have placed it on the scale in two places to indicate the possibility. These subsidiary considerations aside, the

DIAGRAM 2. A continuum showing some of the choices available between compulsion and information by government action, as illustrated by techniques for the settlement of industrial disputes

Information

Compulsion

Above the line (from Information toward Compulsion):

Informal advice from and consultation with government officials

Conciliation

Mediation

"Cooling-off" requirements

Fact-finding boards without power to recommend settlement

Fact-finding boards with power to recommend settlement

Highly organized "voluntary" back-to-work movement supported by local govt., police, businessmen, etc.

President's back-to-work appeal

Below the line:

Compulsory arbitration where no effective means of enforcing the award is at hand

Voluntary arbitration

Compulsory arbitration

Injunction

Militia

Above the line: techniques commonly considered as those of "education," "persuasion," and "appeals to reason."
Below the line: techniques commonly considered as those of "power," "coercion," and "orders."

important fact is simply that the available techniques offer almost any combination of information and compulsion that might be desired.

Diagram 3 illustrates the gradations possible in what are sometimes called direct and indirect controls over the level of employment and spending. Typically stabilization policy makes heavy use of indirect control, as, for example, in the manipulation of bank reserve requirements or the control of private spending through variations in government expenditure. On the other hand, it is possible to bring business spending decisions under governmental command by nationalization of industry, licensing of investment, and other direct controls over the individual decisions of named persons or enterprises. Again, however, a range of alternatives connects the two extremes by easy gradations. If it is not already obvious, it is worth pointing out that the choice of one technique for one sector of the economy does not ordinarily preclude a wide choice among other techniques in another sector. This fact is apparent from a mere inspection of the techniques scaled in Diagram 3, but the same is true for the techniques on the other scales.

Diagram 4 represents choices between voluntary and compulsory organizations for a variety of purposes, an illustration which should make clear that policy is never restricted to the simple choice between calling upon "government" to perform a given function and leaving its performance, on the other hand, to a "private" group. The separation of techniques above and below the line is an incidental reminder that private organizations may be as compulsory as government organizations. The comments on the earlier diagrams should make the meaning of this diagram, as well as of Diagram 5, sufficiently clear without further comment. Diagram 5 is an attempt to show the gradation of choice between procedures closely supervised by central government officials and those possessing a high degree of autonomy. Since government is often widely identified with prescription and private organization with autonomy, a wide range of autonomy-prescription combinations is revealing. The number of these diagrams can be increased indefinitely both by examining other kinds of choices and by examining the same kinds of choices with respect to other problems or goals.

Whether the rapidity of innovation in new techniques of con-

DIAGRAM 3. A continuum showing some of the choices available between direct and indirect controls, as illustrated in techniques to control the level of employment and spending

Direct Control									Indirect Control
Nationalization permitting directives on investment Variations in public expenditures	Licensing of private investment	Antitrust	Variations in grants-in-aid to state and local govts.	Regulation of terms of credit in private transactions, as in installment buying	Appeals to business on price policy or to unions on wage policies	Bond sales to consumers	Taxes and subsidies	Manipulation of interest rate and central bank policy	Secondary effect of public expenditures

DIAGRAM 4. A continuum showing some of the choices available between voluntary and compulsory organizations

Voluntary									Compulsory
Advisory councils	Civil service	Contracting members of Agric. Adj. Admin.	NRA code groups	Land-use planning districts	Tax districts	Municipality	An American state	Social security systems	The nation-state
Small private clubs	Political parties / Pressure groups	Guilds and syndicates	Professional and business organizations	Union with maintenance-of-membership rule	Closed-shop union	Class and status groups	Guilds and syndicates		
			Unions		Business firm where annuity is lost on separation	Business groups with delegated govt. power: e.g., newsprint users in Great Britain			

Above the line: organizations commonly thought of as governmental.
Below the line: organizations commonly thought of as private.

DIAGRAM 5. A continuum showing some of the choices available among kinds of public agencies according to the degree to which the agency's operations are prescribed by a hierarchical superior

Autonomy → Prescription

	British governmental agencies (above the line)	U.S. governmental agencies (below the line)
1	BBC	Autonomous agencies: e.g., trustees of the New Haven commons
2	Coal Board	Semi-autonomous agencies such as the Port of New York Authority
3	Local govt.	Atomic Energy Commission
4	Bank of England	Supreme Court
5	Organization and Management Division, Treasury	TVA — Securities and Exchange Commission
6	Courts	Regulatory commissions
7	Cabinet	Reclamation Bureau — Interstate Commerce Commission
8	Secretariat	Budget Bureau
9	General Acctg. Office	Unemployment compensation
10	Ministry of Pensions	Veterans' Administration
11	Stationery Office	

Above the line: British governmental agencies.
Below the line: U.S. governmental agencies.
Placement of British and American agencies is not comparable.

trol is or is not the greatest political revolution of our times, techniques and not "isms" are the kernel of rational social action in the Western world. Both socialism and capitalism are dead. The politico-economic systems of the United States and of Britain differ in important respects, to be sure; yet both major parties in both countries are attacking their economic problems with fundamentally the same kinds of techniques. Ideological differences between the parties in each country and between the countries themselves are significant in affecting the choice of techniques; but policy in any case is technique-minded, and it is becoming increasingly difficult in both countries to argue policy in terms of the mythical grand alternatives.

The Scope and Bias of the Pressure System

E. E. SCHATTSCHNEIDER

E. E. Schattschneider is Professor of Government Emeritus at Wesleyan University. This article is from his book, The Semi-Sovereign People, *published in 1960.*

THE SCOPE of conflict is an aspect of the scale of political organization and the extent of political competition. The size of the constituencies being mobilized, the inclusiveness or exclusiveness of the conflicts people expect to develop have a bearing on all theories about how politics is or should be organized. In other words, nearly all theories about politics have something to do with the question of who can get into the fight and who is to be excluded.

Every regime is a testing ground for theories of this sort. More than any other system American politics provides the raw materials for testing the organizational assumptions of two contrasting kinds of politics, *pressure politics* and *party politics*. The concepts that underlie these forms of politics constitute the raw stuff of a general theory of political action. The basic issue between the two patterns of organization is one of size and scope of conflict; pressure groups are small-scale organizations while political parties are very large-scale organizations. One need not be surprised, therefore, that the partisans of large-scale and small-scale organizations differ passionately, because the outcome of the political game depends on the scale on which it is played.

To understand the controversy about the scale of political organization it is necessary first to take a look at some theories about interest-group politics. Pressure groups have played a remarkable role in American politics, but they have played an even more remarkable role in American political theory. Considering the political condition of the country in the first third of the twentieth century, it was probably inevitable that the discussion of special interest pressure groups should lead to development of "group" theories of politics in which an attempt is made to explain everything in terms of group activity, i.e., an attempt to formulate a universal group theory. Since one of the best ways to test an idea is to ride it into the ground, political theory has unquestionably been improved by the heroic attempt to create a political universe revolving about the group. Now that we have a number of drastic statements of the group theory of politics pushed to a great extreme, we ought to be able to see what the limitations of the idea are.

Political conditions in the first third of the present century were extremely hospitable to the idea. The role of business in the strongly sectional Republican system from 1896 to 1932 made the dictatorship of business seem to be a part of the eternal order of things. Moreover, the regime as a whole seemed to be so stable that questions about the survival of the American community did not arise. The general interests of the community were easily overlooked under these circumstances.

Nevertheless, in spite of the excellent and provocative scholarly work done by Beard, Latham, Truman, Leiserson, Dahl, Lindblom, Laski and others, the group theory of politics is beset with difficulties. The difficulties are theoretical, growing in part out of sheer overstatements of the idea and in part out of some confusion about the nature of modern government.

One difficulty running through the literature of the subject results from the attempt to explain *everything* in terms of the group theory. On general grounds it would be remarkable indeed if a single hypothesis explained everything about so complex a subject as American politics. Other difficulties have grown out of the fact that group concepts have been stated in terms so universal that the subject seems to have no shape or form.

The question is: Are pressure groups the universal basic ingredient of all political situations, and do they explain everything? To answer this question it is necessary to review a bit of rudimentary political theory.

Two modest reservations might be made merely to test the group dogma. We might clarify our ideas if (1) we explore more fully the possibility of making a distinction between public interest groups and special-interest groups and (2) if we distinguished between organized and unorganized groups. These reservations do not disturb the main body of group theory, but they may be useful when we attempt to define general propositions more precisely. If both of these distinctions can be validated, we may get hold of something that has scope and limits and is capable of being defined. The awkwardness of a discussion of political phenomena in terms of universals is that the subject has no beginning or end; it is impossible to distinguish one subject from another or to detect the bias of the forces involved because scope and bias are aspects of the limitations of the subject. It cannot really be said that we have seen a subject until we have seen its outer limits and thus are able to draw a line between one subject and another.

We might begin to break the problem into its component parts by exploring the distinction between public and private interests. If we can validate this distinction, we shall have established one of the boundaries of the subject.

As a matter of fact, the distinction between *public* and *private interests* is a thoroughly respectable one; it is one of the oldest known to political theory. In the literature of the subject the public interest refers to general or common interests shared by all or by substantially all members of the community. Presumably no community exists unless there is some kind of community of interests, just as there is no nation without some notion of national interests. If it is really impossible to distinguish between private and public interests the group theorists have produced a revolution in political thought so great that it is impossible to foresee its consequences. For this reason the distinction ought to be explored with great care.

At a time when nationalism is described as one of the most dynamic forces in the world, it should not be difficult to understand that national interests actually do exist. It is necessary only to consider the proportion of the American budget devoted to national defense to realize that the common interest in national survival is a great one. Measured in dollars this interest is one of the biggest things in the world. Moreover, it is difficult to describe this interest as special. The diet on which the American leviathan feeds is something more than a jungle of disparate special interests. In the literature of democratic theory the body of common agreement found in the community is known as the "consensus" without which it is believed that no democratic system can survive.

The reality of the common interest is suggested by demonstrated capacity of the community to survive. There must be something that holds people together.

In contrast with the common interests are the special interests. The implication of this term is that these are interests shared by only a few people or a fraction of the community; they *exclude* others and may be *adverse* to them. A special interest is exclusive in about the same way as private property is exclusive. In a complex society it is not surprising that there are some interests that are shared by all or substantially all members of the community and some interests that are not shared so widely. The distinction is useful precisely because conflicting claims are made by people about the nature of their interests in controversial matters.

Perfect agreement within the community is not always possible, but an interest may be said to have become public when it is shared so widely as to be substantially universal. Thus the difference between 99 per cent agreement and perfect agreement is not so great that it becomes necessary to argue that all interests are special, that the interests of the 99 per cent are as special as the interests of the 1 per cent. For example, the law is probably doing an adequate job of defining the public interest in domestic tranquility despite the fact that there is nearly always one dissenter at every hanging. That is, the law defines the public interest in spite of the fact that there may be some outlaws.

Since one function of theory is to explain reality, it is reasonable to add that it is a good deal easier to explain what is going on in politics by making a distinction between public and private interests than it is to attempt to explain *everything* in terms of special interests. The attempt to prove that all interests are special forces us into circumlocutions such as those involved in the argument that people have special interests in the common good. The argument can be made, but it seems a long way around to avoid a useful distinction.

What is to be said about the argument that the distinction between public and special interests is "subjective" and is therefore "unscientific"?

All discussion of interests, special as well as general, refers to the motives, desires and intentions of people. In this sense the whole discussion of interests is subjective. We have made progress in the study of politics because people have observed some kind of relation between the political behavior of people and certain wholly impersonal data concerning their ownership of property, income, economic status, professions and the like. All that we know about interests, private as well as public, is based on inferences of this sort. Whether the distinction in any given case is valid depends on the evidence and on the kinds of inferences drawn from the evidence. . . .

All public discussion is addressed to the general community. To describe the conflict of special-interest groups as a form of politics means that the conflict has become generalized, has become a matter involving the broader public. In the nature of things a *political conflict among special interests is never restricted to the groups most immediately interested.* Instead, it is an appeal (initiated by relatively small numbers of people) for the support of vast numbers of people who are sufficiently remote to have a somewhat different perspective on the controversy.

The distinction between public and special interests is an indispensable tool for the study of politics. To abolish the distinction is to make a shambles of political science by treating things that are different as if they were alike. The kind of distinction made here is a commonplace of all literature dealing with human society, but *if we accept it we have established one of the outer limits of the subject;* we have split the world of interests in half and have taken one step toward defining the scope of this kind of political conflict.

We can now examine the second distinction, the distinction between organized and unorganized groups. The question here is not whether the distinction can be made but whether or not it is worth making. Organization has been described as "merely a stage or degree of interaction" in the development of a group.

The proposition is a good one, but what conclusions do we draw from it? We do not dispose of the matter by calling the distinction between organized and unorganized groups a "mere" difference of degree because some of the greatest differences in the world are differences of degree. As far as special-interest politics is concerned the implication to be avoided is that a few workmen who habitually stop at a corner saloon for a glass of beer are essentially the same as the United States Army because the difference between them is merely one of degree. At this point we have a distinction that makes a difference. The distinction between organized and unorganized groups is worth making because it ought to alert us against an analysis which begins as a general group theory of politics but ends with a defense of pressure politics as inherent, universal, permanent and inevitable.

This kind of confusion comes from the loosening of categories involved in the universalization of group concepts.

Since the beginning of intellectual history, scholars have sought to make progress in their work by distinguishing between things that are unlike and by dividing their subject matter into categories to examine them more intelligently. It is something of a novelty, therefore, when group theorists reverse this process by discussing their subject in terms so universal that they wipe out all categories, because this is the dimension in which it is least possible to understand anything.

If we are able, therefore, to distinguish between public and private interests and between organized and unorganized groups we have marked out the major boundaries of the subject; *we have given the subject shape and scope*. We are now in a position to attempt to define the area we want to explore. Having cut the pie into four pieces, we can now appropriate the piece we want and leave the rest to someone else. For a multitude of reasons *the most likely field of study is that of the organized, special-interest groups*. The advantage of concentrating on organized groups is that they are known, identifiable and recognizable. The advantage of concentrating on special-interest groups is that they have one important characteristic in common: they are all exclusive. This piece of the pie (the organized special-interest groups) we shall call the *pressure system*. The pressure system has boundaries we can define; we can fix its scope and make an attempt to estimate its bias. . . .

Broadly, the pressure system has an upper-class bias. There is overwhelming evidence that participation in voluntary organizations is related to upper social and economic status; the rate of participation is much higher in the upper strata than it is elsewhere. . . .

The bias of the system is shown by the fact that *even nonbusiness organizations reflect an upper-class tendency*. The obverse side of the coin is that large areas of the population appear to be wholly outside of the system of private organization. . . .

There is a great wealth of data supporting the proposition that participation in private associations exhibits a class bias.

The class bias of associational activity gives meaning to the limited scope of the pressure system, because *scope and bias are aspects of the same tendency*. The data raise a serious question about the validity of the proposition that special-interest groups are a universal form of political organization reflecting *all* interests. As a matter of fact, to suppose that everyone participates in pressure-group activity and that all interests get themselves organized in the pressure system is to destroy the meaning of this form of politics. The pressure system makes sense only as the political instrument of a segment of the community. It gets results by being selective and biased; *if everybody got into the act the unique advantages of this form of organization would be destroyed, for it is possible that if all interests could be mobilized the result would be a stalemate.*

Special-interest organizations are most easily formed when they deal with small numbers of individuals who are acutely aware of their exclusive interests. To describe the conditions of pressure-group organization in this way is, however, to say that it is primarily a business phenomenon. Aside from a few very large organizations (the churches, organized labor, farm organizations, and veterans' organizations) the residue is a small segment of the population. *Pressure politics is essentially the politics of small groups.*

The vice of the groupist theory is that it conceals the most significant aspects of the system. The flaw in the pluralist heaven is that the heavenly chorus sings with a strong upper-class accent. Probably about 90 per cent of the people cannot get into the pressure system.

The notion that the pressure system is automatically representative of the whole community is a myth fostered by the universalizing tendency of modern group theories. *Pressure politics is a selective process* ill designed to serve diffuse interests. The system is skewed, loaded and unbalanced in favor of a fraction of a minority.

On the other hand, pressure tactics are not remarkably successful in mobilizing general interests. When pressure-group organizations attempt to represent the interests of large numbers of people, they are usually able to reach only a small segment of their constituencies. Only a chemical trace of the fifteen million Negroes in the United States belong to the National Association for the Advancement of Colored People. Only one five-hundredths of 1 per cent of American women belong to the League of Women Voters, only one sixteenth-hundredths of 1 per cent of the consumers belong to the National Consumers' League, and only 6 per cent of American automobile drivers belong to the American Automobile Association, while about 15 per cent of the veterans belong to the American Legion.

The competing claims of pressure groups and political parties for the loyalty of the American public revolve about the difference between the results likely to be achieved by small-scale and large-scale political organization. Inevitably, the outcome of pressure politics and party politics will be vastly different.

A CRITIQUE OF GROUP THEORIES OF POLITICS

It is extremely unlikely that the vogue of group theories of politics would have attained its present status if its basic assumptions had not been first established by some concept of economic determinism. The economic interpretation of politics has always appealed to those political philosophers who have sought a single prime mover, a sort of philosopher's stone of political science around which to organize their ideas. The search for a single, ultimate cause has something to do with the attempt to explain *everything* about politics in terms of group concepts. The logic of economic determinism is to *identify the origins of conflict and to assume the conclusion.* This kind of thought has some of the earmarks of an illusion. The somnambulatory quality of thinking in this field appears also in the tendency of research to deal only with successful pressure campaigns or the willingness of scholars to be satisfied with having placed pressure groups on the scene of the crime without following through to see if the effect can really be attributed to the cause. What makes this kind of thinking remarkable is the fact that in political contests there are as many failures as there are successes. Where in the literature of pressure politics are the failures?

Students of special-interest politics need a more sophisticated set of intellectual tools than they have developed thus far. The theoretical problem involved in the search for a single cause is that all power relations in a democracy are reciprocal. Trying to find the original cause is like trying to find the first wave of the ocean.

Can we really assume that we know all that is to be known about a conflict if we understand its *origins?* Everything we know

about politics suggests that a conflict is likely to change profoundly as it becomes political. It is a rare individual who can
confront his antagonists without changing his opinions to some
degree. Everything changes once a conflict gets into the political
arena—*who* is involved, *what* the conflict is about, the resources
available, etc. It is extremely difficult to predict the outcome of
a fight by watching its beginning because we do not even know
who else is going to get into the conflict. The logical consequence
of the exclusive emphasis on the determinism of the private
origins of conflict is to assign zero value to the political process.

The very expression "pressure politics" invites us to misconceive the role of special-interest groups in politics. The word
"pressure" implies the use of some kind of force, a form of in-
timidation, something other than reason and information, to in-
duce public authorities to act against their own best judgment.
In Latham's famous statement the legislature is described as a
"referee" who "ratifies" and "records" the "balance of power"
among the contending groups.

It is hard to imagine a more effective way of saying that Congress has no mind or force of its own or that Congress is unable
to invoke new forces that might alter the equation.

Actually the outcome of political conflict is not like the "resultant" of opposing forces in physics. To assume that the forces
in a political situation could be diagrammed as a physicist might
diagram the resultant of opposing physical forces is to wipe the
slate clean of all remote, general and public considerations for
the protection of which civil societies have been instituted.

Moreover, the notion of "pressure" distorts the image of the
power relations involved. *Private conflicts are taken into the public arena precisely because someone wants to make certain that*

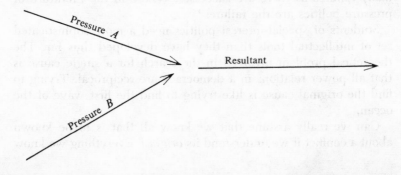

the power ratio among the private interests most immediately involved shall not prevail. To treat a conflict as a mere test of the strength of the private interests is to leave out the most significant factors. This is so true that it might indeed be said that the only way to preserve private power ratios is to keep conflicts out of the public arena.

The assumption that it is only the "interested" who count ought to be re-examined in view of the foregoing discussion. The tendency of the literature of pressure politics has been to neglect the low-tension force of large numbers because it *assumes that the equation of forces is fixed at the outset.*

Given the assumptions made by the group theorists, the attack on the idea of the majority is completely logical. The assumption is that conflict is monopolized narrowly by the parties immediately concerned. There is no room for a majority when conflict is defined so narrowly. It is a great deficiency of the group theory that it has found no place in the political system for the majority. The force of the majority is of an entirely different order of magnitude, something not to be measured by pressure-group standards.

Instead of attempting to exterminate all political forms, organizations and alignments that do not qualify as pressure groups, would it not be better to attempt to make a synthesis, covering the whole political system and finding a place for all kinds of political life?

One possible synthesis of pressure politics and party politics might be produced by *describing politics as the socialization of conflict.* That is to say, the political process is a sequence: conflicts are initiated by highly motivated, high-tension groups so directly and immediately involved that it is difficult for them to see the justice of competing claims. As long as the conflicts of these groups remain *private* (carried on in terms of economic competition, reciprocal denial of goods and services, private negotiations and bargaining, struggles for corporate control or competition for membership), no political process is initiated. Conflicts become political only when an attempt is made to involve the wider public. Pressure politics might be described as a stage in the socialization of conflict. This analysis makes pressure politics an integral part of all politics, including party politics.

One of the characteristic points of origin of pressure politics is a breakdown of the discipline of the business community. The flight to government is perpetual. Something like this is likely to happen wherever there is a point of contact between competing power systems. It is the *losers in intrabusiness conflict who seek redress from public authority. The dominant business interests resist appeals to the government.* The role of the government as the patron of the defeated private interest sheds light on its function as the critic of private power relations.

Since the contestants in private conflicts are apt to be unequal in strength, it follows that *the most powerful special interests want private settlements* because they are able to dictate the outcome as long as the conflict remains private. If *A* is a hundred times as strong as *B* he does not welcome the intervention of a third party because he expects to impose his own terms on *B;* he wants to isolate *B.* He is especially opposed to the intervention of public authority, because public authority represents the most overwhelming form of outside intervention. Thus, if $\dfrac{A}{B} = \dfrac{100}{1}$, it is obviously not to *A*'s advantage to involve a third party a million times as strong as *A* and *B* combined. Therefore, it is the weak, not the strong, who appeal to public authority for relief. It is the weak who want to socialize conflict, i.e., to involve more and more people in the conflict until the balance of forces is changed. In the school yard it is not the bully, but the defenseless smaller boys who "tell the teacher." When the teacher intervenes the balance of power in the school yard is apt to change drastically. It is the function of public authority to *modify private power relations by enlarging the scope of conflict.* Nothing could be more mistaken than to suppose that public authority merely registers the dominance of the strong over the weak. The mere existence of public order has already ruled out a great variety of forms of private pressure. Nothing could be more confusing than to suppose that the refugees from the business community who come to Congress for relief and protection *force* Congress to do their bidding.

Evidence of the truth of this analysis may be seen in the fact that the big private interests do not necessarily win if they are involved in public conflicts with petty interests. The image of the lobbyists as primarily the agents of big business is not easy to support on the fact of the record of congressional hearings, for example. The biggest corporations in the country tend to avoid the arena in which pressure groups and lobbyists fight it out before congressional committees. To describe this process exclusively in terms of an effort of business to intimidate congressmen is to misconceive what is actually going on.

It is probably a mistake to assume that pressure politics is the typical or even the most important relation between government and business. The pressure group is by no means the perfect instrument of the business community. What does big business want? The *winners* in intrabusiness strife want (1) to be let alone (they want autonomy) and (2) to preserve the solidarity of the business community. For these purposes pressure politics is not a wholly satisfactory device. The most elementary considerations of strategy call for the business community to develop some kind of common policy more broadly based than any special-interest group is likely to be.

The political influence of business depends on the kind of solidarity that, on the one hand, leads all business to rally to the support of *any* businessman in trouble with the government, and on the other hand, keeps internal business disputes out of the public arena. In this system businessmen resist the impulse to attack each other in public and discourage the efforts of individual members of the business community to take intrabusiness conflicts into politics.

The attempt to mobilize a united front of the whole business community does not resemble the classical concept of pressure politics. The logic of business politics is to keep peace within the business community by supporting as far as possible all claims that business groups make for themselves. The tendency is to support all businessmen who have conflicts with the government and support all businessmen in conflict with labor. In this way *special-interest politics can be converted into party policy.* The search is for a broad base of political mobilization grounded on the strategic need for political organization on a wider scale than is possible in the case of the historical pressure group. Once the business community begins to think in terms of a larger scale of political organization the Republican party looms large in business politics.

It is a great achievement of American democracy that business has been forced to form a political organization designed to win elections, i.e., has been forced to compete for power in the widest arena in the political system. On the other hand, *the power of the Republican party to make terms with business rests on the fact that business cannot afford to be isolated.*

The Republican party has played a major role in *the political organization of the business community,* a far greater role than many students of politics seem to have realized. The influence of business in the Republican party is great, but it is never absolute because business is remarkably dependent on the party. The business community is too small, it arouses too much antagonism, and its aims are too narrow to win the support of a popular majority. The political education of business is a function of the Republican party that can never be done so well by anyone else.

In the management of the political relations of the business community, the Republican party is much more important than any combination of pressure groups ever could be. The success of special interests in Congress is due less to the "pressure" exerted by these groups than it is due to the fact that Republican members of Congress are committed in advance to a general probusiness attitude. The notion that business groups coerce Republican congressmen into voting for their bills underestimates the whole Republican posture in American politics.

It is not easy to manage the political interests of the business community because there is a perpetual stream of losers in intrabusiness conflicts who go to the government for relief and protection. It has not been possible therefore to maintain perfect solidarity, and when solidarity is breached the government is involved almost automatically. The fact that business has not become hopelessly divided and that it has retained great influence in American politics has been due chiefly to the over-all mediating role played by the Republican party. There has never been a pressure group or a combination of pressure groups capable of performing this function.

Distribution, Regulation, Redistribution: The Functions of Government

Theodore J. Lowi is Associate Professor of Political Science at the University of Chicago. This selection is taken from an extended review of Raymond Bauer, Ithiel de Sola Pool, and Lewis A. Dexter, American Business and Public Policy.

IN THE long run, all governmental policies may be considered redistributive, because in the long run some people pay in taxes more than they receive in services. Or, all may be thought regulatory because, in the long run, a governmental decision on the use of resources can only displace a private decision about the same resource or at least reduce private alternatives about the resource. But politics works in the short run, and in the short run certain kinds of government decisions can be made without regard to limited resources. Policies of this kind are called "distributive," a term first coined for nineteenth-century land policies, but easily extended to include most contemporary public land and resource policies; rivers and harbors ("pork barrel") programs; defense procurement and research and development programs; labor, business, and agricultural "clientele" services; and the traditional tariff. Distributive policies are characterized by the ease with which they can be disaggregated and dispensed unit by small unit, each unit more or less in isolation from other units and from any general rule. "Patronage" in the fullest meaning of the word can be taken as a synonym for "distributive." These are policies that are virtually not policies at all but are highly individualized decisions that only by accumulation can be called a policy. They are policies in which the indulged and the deprived, the loser and the recipient, need never come into direct confrontation. Indeed, in many instances of distributive policy, the deprived cannot as a class be identified, because the most influential among them can be accommodated by further disaggregation of the stakes.

Regulatory policies are also specific and individual in their impact, but they are not capable of the almost infinite amount of disaggregation typical of distributive policies. Although the laws are stated in general terms ("Arrange the transportation system artistically." "Thou shalt not show favoritism in pricing."), the impact of regulatory decisions is clearly one of directly raising costs and/or reducing or expanding the alternatives of private individuals ("Get off the grass!" "Produce kosher if you advertise kosher!"). Regulatory policies are distinguishable from distributive in that in the short run the regulatory decision involves a direct choice as to who will be indulged and who deprived. Not all applicants for a single television channel or an overseas air route can be propitiated. Enforcement of an unfair labor practice on the part of management weakens management in its dealings with labor. So, while implementation is firm-by-firm and case-by-case, policies cannot be disaggregated to the level of the individual or the single firm (as in distribution), because individual decisions must be made by application of a general rule and therefore become interrelated within the broader standards of law. Decisions cumulate among all individuals affected by the law in roughly the same way. Since the most stable lines of perceived common impact are the basic sectors of the economy, regulatory decisions are cumulative largely along sectoral lines; regulatory policies are usually disaggregable only down to the sector level.

Redistributive policies are like regulatory policies in the sense that relations among broad categories of private individuals are involved and, hence, individual decisions must be interrelated. But on all other counts there are great differences in the nature of impact. The categories of impact are much broader, approaching social classes. They are, crudely speaking, haves and have-nots, bigness and smallness, bourgeoisie and proletariat. The aim involved is not use of property but property itself, not equal treatment but equal possession, not behavior but being. The fact that our income tax is in reality only mildly redistributive does not alter the fact of the aims and the stakes involved in income tax policies. The same goes for our various "welfare state" programs, which are redistributive only for those who entered retirement or unemployment rolls without having contributed at all. The nature of a redistributive issue is not determined by the outcome of a battle over how redistributive a policy is going to be. Expectations about what it *can* be, what it threatens to be, are determinative.

ARENAS OF POWER

Once one posits the general tendency of these areas of policy or governmental activity to develop characteristic political structures, a number of hypotheses become compelling. And when the various hypotheses are accumulated, the general contours of each of the three arenas begin quickly to resemble, respectively, the three "general" theories of political process. The arena that develops around distributive policies is best characterized in the terms of E. E. Schattschneider's findings on the politics of tariff legislation in the nineteen-twenties. The regulatory arena corresponds to the pluralist school,[1] and the school's general notions are found to be limited pretty much to this one arena. The redistributive arena most closely approximates, with some adaptation, an elitist view of the political process.

(1) The distributive arena can be identified in considerable detail from Schattschneider's case-study alone.[2] What he and his pluralist successors did not see was that the traditional structure of tariff politics is also in largest part the structure of politics of all those diverse policies identified earlier as distributive. The arena is "pluralistic" only in the sense that a large number of small, intensely organized interests are operating. In fact, there is even greater multiplicity of participants here than the pressure-group model can account for, because essentially it is a politics of every man for himself. The single person and the single firm are the major activists.

Although a generation removed, Schattschneider's conclusions about the politics of the Smoot-Hawley Tariff are almost one-for-one applicable to rivers and harbors and land development policies, tax exemptions, defense procurement, area redevelopment, and government "services." Since there is no real basis for discriminating between those who should and those who should not

1. [The "pluralist school" of American political science contends that public policy outcomes can be largely explained by looking at the pattern of group activity. Some treat government as merely the recorder of group triumphs. Others treat governmental units or groups themselves. *Editor*]

2. E. E. Schattschneider, *Politics, Pressures, and the Tariff* (Hamden, Conn.: Shoe String, 1935).

be protected [indulged], says Schattschneider, Congress seeks political support by "giving a limited protection [indulgence] to all interests strong enough to furnish formidable resistance." Decision-makers become "responsive to considerations of equality, consistency, impartiality, uniformity, precedent, and moderation, however formal and insubstantial these may be." Furthermore, a "policy that is so hospitable and catholic . . . disorganizes the opposition."

When a billion-dollar issue can be disaggregated into many millions of nickel-dime items and each item can be dealt with without regard to the others, multiplication of interests and of access is inevitable, and so is reduction of conflict. All of this has the greatest bearing on the relations among participants and, therefore, the "power structure." Indeed, coalitions must be built to pass legislation and "make policy," but what of the nature and basis of the coalitions? In the distributive arena, political relationships approximate what Schattschneider called "mutual non-interference"—"a mutuality under which it is proper for each to seek duties [indulgences] for himself but improper and unfair to oppose duties [indulgences] sought by others." In the area of rivers and harbors, references are made to "pork barrel" and "log-rolling," but these colloquialisms have not been taken sufficiently seriously. A log-rolling coalition is not one forged of conflict, compromise, and tangential interest but, on the contrary, one composed of members who have absolutely nothing in common; and this is possible because the "pork barrel" is a container for unrelated items. This is the typical form of relationship in the distributive arena.

The structure of these log-rolling relationships leads typically, though not always, to Congress; and the structure is relatively stable because all who have access of any sort usually support whoever are the leaders. And there tend to be "elites" of a peculiar sort in the Congressional committees whose jurisdictions include the subject-matter in question. Until recently, for instance, on tariff matters the House Ways and Means Committee was virtually the government. Much the same can be said for Public Works on rivers and harbors. It is a broker leadership, but "policy" is best understood as cooptation rather than conflict and compromise.

Distributive issues individualize conflict and provide the basis for highly stable coalitions that are virtually irrelevant to the larger policy outcomes; thousands of obscure decisions are merely accumulated into a "policy" of protection or of natural-resources development or of defense subcontracting. Congress did not "give up" the tariff; as the tariff became a matter of regulation (see below), committee elites lost their power to contain the participants because obscure decisions became interrelated, therefore less obscure, and more controversy became built in and unavoidable.

(2) The regulatory arena could hardly be better identified than in the thousands of pages written for the whole polity by the pluralists. But, unfortunately, some translation is necessary to accommodate pluralism to its more limited universe. The regulatory arena appears to be composed of a multiplicity of groups organized around tangential relations or David Truman's "shared attitudes." Within this narrower context of regulatory decisions, one can even go so far as to accept the most extreme pluralist statement that policy tends to be a residue of the interplay of group conflict. This statement can be severely criticized only by use of examples drawn from non-regulatory decisions.

As I argued before, there is no way for regulatory policies to be disaggregated into very large numbers of unrelated items. Because individual regulatory decisions involve direct confrontations of indulged and deprived, the typical political coalition is born of conflict and compromise among tangential interests that usually involve a total sector of the economy. Thus, while the typical basis for coalition in distributive politics is uncommon interests (log-rolling), an entirely different basis is typical in regulatory politics.

Owing to the unrelatedness of issues in distributive politics, the activities of single participants need not be related but rather can be specialized as the situation warrants it. But the relatedness of regulatory issues, at least up to the sector level of the trade association, leads to the containment of all these within the association. When all the stakes are contained in one organization, constituents have no alternative but to fight against each other to shape the policies of that organization or actually to abandon it.

What this suggests is that the typical power structure in regulatory politics is far less stable than that in the distributive arena. Since coalitions form around shared interests, the coalitions will shift as the interests change or as conflicts of interest emerge. With such group-based and shifting patterns of conflict built into every regulatory issue, it is in most cases impossible for a Congressional committee, an administrative agency, a peak association governing board, or a social elite to contain all the participants long enough to establish a stable power elite. Policy outcomes seem inevitably to be the residue remaining after all the reductions of demands by all participants have been made in order to extend support to majority size. But a majority-sized coalition of shared interests on one issue could not possibly be entirely appropriate for some other issue. In regulatory decision-making, relationships among group leadership elements and between them on any one or more points of governmental access are too unstable to form a single policy-making elite. As a consequence, decision-making tends to pass from administrative agencies and Congressional committees to Congress, the place where uncertainties in the policy process have always been settled. Congress as an institution is the last resort for breakdowns in bargaining over policy, just as in the case of parties the primary is a last resort for breakdowns in bargining over nominations. No one leadership group can contain the conflict by an almost infinite subdivision and distribution of the stakes. In the regulatory political process, Congress and the "balance of power" seem to play the classic role attributed to them by the pluralists.

Beginning with reciprocity in the 1930's, the tariff began to lose its capacity for infinite disaggregation because it slowly underwent redefinition, moving away from its purely domestic significance towards that of an instrument of international politics. In brief, the tariff, especially following World War II and our assumption of peace time international leadership, became a means of regulating the domestic economy for international purposes. The significant feature here is not the international but the regulatory part of the redefinition. As the process of redefinition took place, a number of significant shifts in power relations took place as well, because it was no longer possible to deal with each dutiable item in isolation. Everything in Bauer, Pool, and Dexter points toward the expansion of relationships to the level of the sector. The political problem of the South was the concentration of textile industry there. Coal, oil, and rails came closer and closer to coalition. The final shift came with the 1962 Trade Expansion

Act, which enabled the President for the first time to deal with broad categories (to the sector) rather than individual commodities.

Certain elements of distributive politics remain, for two obvious reasons. First, there are always efforts on the part of political leaders to disaggregate policies because this is the best way to spread the patronage and to avoid conflict. (Political actors, like economic actors, probably view open competition as a necessary evil or a last resort to be avoided at almost any cost.) Second, until 1962, the basic tariff law and schedules were still contained in the Smoot-Hawley Act. This act was amended by Reciprocal Trade but only to the extent of allowing negotiated reductions rather than reductions based on comparative costs. Until 1962, tariff politics continued to be based on commodity-by-commodity transactions, and thus until then tariff coalitions could be based upon individual firms (or even branches of large and diversified firms) and log-rolling, unrelated interests. The escape clause and peril point were maintained in the 1950's so that transactions could be made on individual items even within reciprocity. And the coalitions of strange bedfellows continued: "Offered the proper coalition, they both [New England textiles and Eastern railroads] might well have been persuaded that their interest was in the opposite direction."

But despite the persistence of certain distributive features, the true nature of tariff in the 1960's emerges as regulatory policy with a developing regulatory arena. Already we can see some changes in Congress even more clearly than the few already observed in the group structure. Out of a committee (House Ways and Means) elite, we can see the emergence of Congress in a pluralist setting. Even as early as 1954–1955, the compromises eventually ratified by Congress were worked out, not in committee through direct cooptation of interests, but in the Randall Commission, a collection of the major interests in conflict. Those issues that could not be thrashed out through the "group process" also could not be thrashed out in committee but had to pass on to Congress and the floor. After 1954 the battle centered on major categories of goods (even to the extent of a textile management-union entente) and the battle took place more or less openly on the floor. The weakening of the Ways and Means Committee as the tariff elite is seen in the fact that in 1955 Chairman Jere

Cooper was unable to push a closed rule through. The Rules Committee, "in line with tradition," granted a closed rule but the House voted it down 207-178. Bauer, Pool, and Dexter saw this as a victory for protectionism, but it is also evidence of the emerging regulatory arena—arising from the difficulty of containing conflict and policy within the governing committee. The last effort to keep the tariff as a traditional instrument of distributive politics—a motion by Daniel Reed to recommit, with instructions to write in a provision that Tariff Commission rulings under the escape clause be final except where the President finds the national security to be involved—was voted down 206-199. After that, right up to 1962, it was clear that tariff decisions would not be made piecemeal. Tariff became a regulatory policy in 1962; all that remains of distributive politics now are quotas and subsidies for producers of specific commodities injured by general tariff reductions.

(3) Compared particularly with the regulatory area, very few case-studies of redistributive decisions have ever been published. This in itself is a significant datum—which C. Wright Mills attributes to the middle-level character of the issues that have gotten attention. But, whatever the reasons, it reduces the opportunities for elaborating upon and testing the scheme. Most of the propositions to follow are illustrated by a single case, the "welfare state" battle of the 1930's. But this case is a complex of many decisions that became one of the most important acts of policy ever achieved in the United States. A brief review of the facts of the case will be helpful. Other cases will be referred to in less detail from time to time.

As the 1934 mid-term elections approached, pressures for a federal social security system began to mount. The Townsend Plan and the Lundeen Bill had become nationally prominent and were gathering widespread support. Both schemes were severely redistributive, giving all citizens access to government-based insurance as a matter of right. In response, the President created in June of 1934 a Committee on Economic Security (CES) composed of top cabinet members with Secretary of Labor Perkins as chairman. In turn, they set up an Advisory Council and a Technical Board, which held hearings, conducted massive studies, and emerged on January 17, 1935, with a bill. The insiders around the CES were representatives of large industries, business associations, unions, and the most interested government bureaucracies. And the detailed legislative histories reveal that virtually all of the debate was contained within the CES and its committees until a mature bill emerged. Since not all of the major issues had been settled in the CES's bill, its members turned to Congress with far from a common front. But the role of Congress was still not what would have been expected. Except for a short fight over committee jurisdiction (won by the more conservative Finance and Ways and Means committees) the legislative process was extraordinarily quiet, despite the import of the issues. Hearings in both Houses brought forth very few witnesses, and these were primarily CES members supporting the bill, and Treasury Department officials, led by Morgenthau, opposing it with "constructive criticism."

The Congressional battle was quiet because the real struggle was taking place elsewhere, essentially between the Hopkins-Perkins bureaucracies and the Treasury. The changes made in the CES bill had all been proposed by Morgenthau (the most important one being the principle of contribution, which took away the redistributive sting). And the final victory for Treasury and mild redistribution came with the removal of administrative responsibility from both Labor and Hopkins's Federal Emergency Relief Administration. Throughout all of this some public expressions of opinion were to be heard from the peak associations, but their efforts were mainly expended in the quieter proceedings in the bureaucracies. The Congress's role seems largely to have been one of ratifying agreements that arose out of the bureaucracies and the class agents represented there. Revisions attributable to Congress concerned such matters as exceptions in coverage, which are part of the distributive game that Congress plays at every opportunity. The *principle* of the Act was set in an interplay involving (quietly) top executives and business and labor leaders.

With only slight changes in the left-right positions of the participants, the same pattern has been observed in income tax decisions. Professor Stanley S. Surrey notes: "The question, 'Who speaks for tax equity and tax fairness?,' is answered today largely in terms of only the Treasury Department." "Thus, in tax bouts . . . it is the Treasury versus percentage legislation, the Treasury versus capital gains, the Treasury versus this constituent, the Treasury versus that private group. . . . As a consequence, the congressman . . . [sees] a dispute . . . only as a contest between a private group and a government department." Congress, says Surrey, "occupies the role of mediator between the tax views of the executive and the demands of the pressure groups." And when the tax issues "are at a major political level, as are tax rates or personal exemptions, then pressure groups, labor organizations, the Chamber of Commerce, the National Association of Manufacturers, and the others, become concerned." The "average congressman does not basically believe in the present income tax in the upper brackets," but rather than touch the principle he deals in "special hardship" and "penalizing" and waits for decisions on principle to come from abroad. Amidst the 1954–1955 tax controversies, for example, Ways and Means members decided to allow each member one bill to be favorably reported if the bill met with unanimous agreement.

Issues that involve redistribution cut closer than any others along class lines and activate interests in what are roughly class terms. If there is ever any cohesion within the peak associations, it occurs on redistributive issues, and their rhetoric suggests that they occupy themselves most of the time with these. In a ten-year period just before and after, but not including, the war years, the Manufacturers' Association of Connecticut, for example, expressed itself overwhelmingly more often on redistributive than on any other types of issues. Table 1 summarizes the pattern, showing

TABLE 1. Published expressions of Manufacturers' Association of Connecticut on selected issues

	Number of References in Ten-year Period (1934–40, 1946–48)	Per Cent of Favorable References
1. Unspecified regulation	378	7.7
2. Labor relations, general	297	0.0
3. Wages and hours	195	0.5
Total expressions, redistribution	870	
4. Trade practices	119	13.8
5. Robinson-Patman	103	18.4
6. Antitrust	72	26.4
7. Basing points	55	20.0
8. Fair-Trade (Miller-Tydings)	69	45.5
Total expressions, regulation	418	

SOURCE: Lane, *The Regulation of Businessmen* (New Haven, 1953), 38ff. The figures are his; their arrangement is mine.

that expressions on generalized issues involving basic relations between bourgeoisie and proletariat outnumbered expressions on regulation of business practices by 870 to 418, despite the larger number of issues in the latter category. This pattern goes contrary to the one observed by Bauer, Pool, and Dexter in tariff politics, where they discovered, much to their surprise, that self-interest did not activate both "sides" equally. Rather, they found, the concreteness and specificity of protectionist interests activated them much more often and intensely than did the general, ideological position of the liberal-traders. This was true in tariff, as they say, because there the "structure of the communications system favored the propagation of particular demands." But there is also a structure of communications favoring generalized and ideological demands; this structure consists of the peak associations, and it is highly effective when the issues are generalizable. This is the case consistently for redistributive issues, almost never for distributive issues, and only seldom for regulatory issues.

As the pluralists would argue, there will be a vast array of organized interests for any item on the policy agenda. But the relations among the interests and between them and government vary, and the nature of and conditions for this variation are what our political analyses should be concerned with. Let us say, in brief, that on Monday night the big associations meet in agreement and considerable cohesion on "the problem of government," the income tax, the Welfare State. On Tuesday, facing regulatory issues, the big associations break up into their constituent trade and other specialized groups, each prepared to deal with special problems in its own special ways, usually along subject-matter lines. On Wednesday night still another fission takes place as the pork barrel and the other forms of subsidy and policy patronage come under consideration. The parent groups and "catalytic groups" still exist, but by Wednesday night they have little identity. As Bauer, Pool, and Dexter would say, they have preserved their unanimity through overlapping memberships. They gain identity to the extent that they can define the issues in redistributive terms. And when interests in issues are more salient in sectoral or geographic or individual terms, the common or generalized factor will be lost in abstractness and diffuseness. This is what happened to the liberal trade groups in the tariff battles of the 1950's, when "the protectionist position was more firmly grounded in direct business considerations and . . . the liberal-trade position fitted better with the ideology of the times . . ."

Where the peak associations, led by elements of Mr. Mills's power elite, have reality, their resources and access are bound to affect power relations. Owing to their stability and the impasse (or equilibrium) in relations among broad classes of the entire society, the political structure of the redistributive arena seems to be highly stabilized, virtually institutionalized. Its stability, unlike that of the distributive arena, derives from shared interests. But in contrast to the regulatory arena, these shared interests are sufficiently stable and clear and consistent to provide the foundation for ideologies. Table 2 summarizes the hypothesized differences in political relationships drawn above.

Many of the other distinctive characteristics of this arena are related to, perhaps follow from, the special role of the peak associations. The cohesion of peak associations means that the special differences among related but competing groups are likely to be settled long before the policies reach the governmental agenda. In many respects the upperclass directors perform the functions in the redistributive arena that are performed by Congressional committees in the distributive arena and by committees and Congress in the regulatory arena. But the differences are crucial. In distributive policies there are as many "sides" as there are tariff items, bridges and dams to be built, parcels of public land to be given away or leased, and so on. And there are probably as many elites as there are Congressional committees and subcommittees which have jurisdiction over distributive policies. In redistribution, there will never be more than two sides and the sides are clear, stable, and consistent. Negotiation is possible, but only for the purpose of strengthening or softening the impact of redistribution. And there is probably one elite for each side. The elites do not correspond directly to bourgeoisie and proletariat; they are better understood under Wallace Sayre's designation of "money-providing" and "service-demanding" groups. Nonetheless, the basis for coalition is broad, and it centers around those individuals most respected and best known for worth and wealth. If the top leaders did not know each other and develop common perspectives as a result of common schooling, as Mills would argue, these commonalities could easily develop later in life because the kinds of stakes involved in redistributive issues are

Table 2. Arenas and political relationships: a diagrammatic survey

Arena	Primary Political Unit	Relation Among Units	Power Structure	Stability of Structure	Primary Decisional Locus	Implementation
Distribution	Individual, firm, corporation	Log-rolling, mutual non-interference, uncommon interests	Non-conflictual elite with support groups	Stable	Congressional committee and/or agency**	Agency centralized to primary functional unit ("bureau")
Regulation*	Group	"The coalition," shared subject-matter interest, bargaining	Pluralistic, multi-centered, "theory of balance"	Unstable	Congress, in classic role	Agency decentralized from center by "delegation," mixed control
Redistribution	Association	The "peak association," class, ideology	Conflictual elite, i.e., elite and counterelite	Stable	Executive and peak associations	Agency centralized toward top (above "bureau"), elaborate standards

* Given the multiplicity of organized interests in the regulatory arena, there are obviously many cases of successful log-rolling coalitions that resemble the coalitions prevailing in distributive politics. In this respect, the difference between the regulatory and the distributive arenas is thus one of degree. The *predominant* form of coalition in regulatory politics is deemed to be that of common or tangential interest. Although the difference is only one of degree, it is significant because this prevailing type of coalition makes the regulatory arena so much more unstable, unpredictable, and non-elitist ("balance of power"). When we turn to the redistributive arena, however, we find differences of principle in every sense of the word.

** Distributive politics tends to stabilize around an institutional unit. In most cases, it is the Congressional committee (or subcommittee). But in others, particularly in the Department of Agriculture, the focus is the agency or the agency *and* the committee. In the cities, this is the arena where machine domination continues, if machines were in control in the first place.

always the same. So institutionalized does the conflict become that governmental bureaucracies themselves begin to reflect them, as do national party leaders and Administrations. Finally, just as the nature of redistributive policies influences politics towards the centralization and stabilization of conflict, so does it further influence the removal of decision-making from Congress. A decentralized and bargaining Congress can cumulate but it cannot balance, and redistributive policies require complex balancing on a very large scale. What William H. Riker has said of budget-making applies here: ". . . legislative governments cannot endure a budget. Its finances must be totted up by party leaders in the legislature itself. In a complex fiscal system, however, haphazard legislative judgments cannot bring revenue into even rough alignment with supply. So budgeting is introduced—which transfers financial control to the budget maker. . . ." Congress can provide exceptions to principles and it can implement those principles with elaborate standards of implementation as a condition for the concessions that money-providers will make. But the makers of principles of redistribution seem to be the holders of the "command posts."

None of this suggests a power elite such as Mills would have had us believe existed, but it does suggest a type of stable and continual conflict that can only be understood in class terms. The foundation upon which the social-stratification and power-elite school rested, especially when dealing with national power, was so conceptually weak and empirically unsupported that its critics were led to err in the opposite direction by denying the direct relevance of social and institutional positions and the probability of stable decision-making elites. But the relevance of that approach becomes stronger as the scope of its application is reduced and as the standards for identifying the scope are clarified. But this is equally true of the pluralist school and of those approaches based on a "politics of this-or-that policy."

PART TWO   Techniques of Subsidy

From Patchwork to Purpose: The Background of the Employment Act of 1946

LEON H. KEYSERLING

Leon H. Keyserling was a top economic adviser in the Roosevelt and Truman Administrations. He has continued to engage in public debate on economic policy since that time. This article is from Survey Graphic, March 1945.

1. Our unrivaled American aptitude for technological advance, spurred on by the depression years and since driven harder by impulse of total war, has exceeded the most fanciful expectations. The output per man-hour in a grouping of basic industries rose from an index of 100 for 1923–25 to 122 for 1929, to 167 for 1940.

The increase has not been so startling in other industries or in agriculture. Yet if we couple this rising efficiency with reasonably full employment, it has been calculated that (at the 1944 price level) the value of our annual gross national product, which stood at $106 billion in 1929, slumped to $76 billion in 1932, and rose to $115 billion in 1939—will reach $195 to $200 billion by 1950.

Allowing for increases in population, this would mean by 1950 a general output per capita more than 50 percent higher than in the peak "prosperity" year of 1929.

2. If we come near this attainable goal, we can assure the economic upgrading of the average family and at the same time preserve individual initiative, unusual reward for unusual merit, and full incentives to legitimate private risk taking.

Without making it impossible for any to get rich, we can make it unnecessary for any to suffer poverty.

3. These bright prospects have their dismal counterpoint, if the shortcomings of the past pervade the future. So long as our economic system retains its brittleness, the impact of 20 million

veterans and ex-war workers looking for postwar jobs will deal it a shattering blow. That is, one which ultimately might smash us down into a depression as much larger than the depression of the thirties as our effort in this war has been larger than our effort in the last war.

4. Which of these two roads we follow will not be left to fate. It will be a manmade choice, representing a compound of economic policies and programs put into effect by industry, agriculture, labor, and government. Our future is in their hands—or rather, if we will, in our own.

5. In order that this compound of policies and programs achieve optimum results, it is essential that industry, agriculture, labor, and government work together.

This imposes a double obligation upon the Federal Government. As itself the largest single conditioner of our economy as a whole, its actions must be reasonably clear, stable, and thought through to their ultimate implications. It must also take the leadership (for no other agency can) in bringing its own variegated economic activities into harmony (through conference and agreement) with those of private enterprise, organized labor, and of our State and local governments.

For each of these performers to take a proper part in our national symphony of productive effort, there must be a score. Clearly each of them should play the instrument for which his gifts are greatest; yet, if all of them are to keep clear of discord, someone must wield a baton. Such is the tradition of music; but dictation does not fit into the orchestration of democracy.

6. Hence we must find equivalents for score and director if we are to make the music we want to hear. We must have a unifying American economic policy directed toward a common American economic goal.

THE GAP FILLED BY THE BILL

Once we found substantial agreement on such points as these, it would be a far cry from the time when serious men accepted literally that the poor should always be with us; or shook their heads forlornly at the natural and immutable laws of the "dismal sciences."

But even with consensus about what we have and what we

need, there would remain one difficulty that has balked us at every turn. Aside from our war effort, we have not yet arrived at enough fundamental agreements—or even the machinery for achieving them—with respect to the content or the application of an integrated economic policy to carry us where we want to go.

Curiously indeed, in a pragmatic and practical people, we have not developed any device for a continuing inventory of existing and largely disjointed public policies even to measure whether these are working well or badly.

The full employment bill is designed to fill in this gap. It would blend the economic programs of private enterprise and public agencies into one American economic policy headed toward what might be called an American economic goal. No, the bill does not use these terms. The goal stated is simply this:

* * * the existence at all times of sufficient employment opportunities to enable all Americans who have finished their schooling and who do not have full-time housekeeping responsibilities freely to exercise * * * the right to useful, remunerative, regular and full-time employment.

But if we broaden this idea of full employment to include, also, the best utilization of our natural resources and technical skills (this, the bill at least implies) then it may be said that it sets forth as our American postwar objective:

The achievement of the highest levels of production and presumably the highest standards of living that are within our reach.

A goal of this kind, aside from the means of attaining it, would not seem subject to much debate. Nor would there seem much room for questioning the stated policy of the bill that as much of this achievement as possible should be through the medium of private enterprise and other non-Federal undertakings. This course stems soundly from Lincoln's statescraft that

"It is the function of the Government to do for the people only what they need to have done and cannot do for themselves, or cannot do so well, in their separate and individual capacities."

THE CORE OF THE BILL

The measure, as drafted, rapidly get down to earth in the industrial civilization that has sprung up in the United States since Lincoln's time. It designs machinery for formulating such an overall economic policy, for gearing it to such an American postwar objective, and for consecutively evaluating the means used in terms of the ends sought.

Specifically, the bill provides that at the beginning of each regular session of Congress, the President shall transmit a national production and employment budget. This would set forth, in substance, an estimate of what at the time would constitute full employment coupled with an estimate of:

1. How much employment is in prospect as the sum total of all private and other non-Federal undertakings;

2. How far these undertakings will fall short of the yardstick of full employment;

3. What policies the Federal Government can and should utilize to maximize the success of these private and other non-Federal undertakings in achieving full employment; and, as a final supplement,

4. What programs the Federal Government itself needs to undertake to assure full employment. (Present estimates put that at 50 or 60 million jobs.)

The bill contemplates, also, that the President shall from time to time transmit to the Congress information and legislative recommendations bearing upon this national production and employment budget.

On the congressional side, the bill would establish a Joint Committee on the National Production and Employment Budget. This, in turn, would be composed of the chairman and ranking minority members of the Senate Committees on Appropriations, Banking and Currency, Education and Labor, and Finance, and seven additional Members of the Senate appointed by the President of the Senate. It would include, also, the chairmen and ranking minority members of the House Committees on Appropriations, Banking and Currency, Labor, and Ways and Means, and seven additional Members of the House appointed by the Speaker. Party representation on the joint committee would reflect automatically the relative membership of the majority and minority parties.

The bill provides further that the joint committee shall study this new type of budget transmitted by the President, and by March 1 shall report its findings and recommendations to the

Senate and the House, together with a joint resolution setting forth for the ensuing fiscal year a general policy to serve as guide to the committees on Capitol Hill dealing with related legislation.

THE PLACE OF THE BILL IN OUR THINKING

It can safely be said that no future historian will be able to date the decline of the Republic from the introduction of this bill. It proposes no redistribution of functions between the Congress and the President. It fastens upon no single economic program or panacea for producing full employment, nor does it introduce specific economic measures that have not now been tried out. It involves neither socialization nor nationalization of anything that is now privately owned or operated.

So far as philosophy goes, the bill preaches neither the expansion of governmental functions nor the contraction of voluntary initiative. To the contrary, it explicitly requires that every effort be made to enlarge our system of private enterprise as our first and longest front against unemployment.

As a second line of defense, the bill contemplates that, by some method, the Government shall provide jobs for those who want work when all other methods have failed to employ them. But this residual responsibility of government by the people, for the people, was itself put forward [in the 1944 presidential campaign] with equal fervor by Franklin D. Roosevelt and Thomas E. Dewey.

What is more—two considerations that have not always been uppermost in the past—the bill requires that jobs provided through direct public action shall be tested in terms of their effect upon stimulating private enterprise and in terms of the value of their end products.

More difficult to allay may be trepidation that a thoroughgoing national policy to assure full employment would tend toward the spread of bureaucracy, toward public control, and operation in an ever-increasing area of economic activity.

Wise application of the act would pull strongly in exactly the opposite direction. Let us suppose, for example, that a national production and employment budget had been in effect during a period of reasonably high employment before 1929. One factor entering into that fall's crisis was the failure of mass purchasing power to keep pace with productive capacity. Other factors were rampant speculation in securities and, in reaction to this, the psychology of business fear and contraction which came to a head in the stock market crash.

Under a national production and employment budget, depressive tendencies would have been registered through its continuing annual inventories—long before the country was thrown into the spiral of depression.

By 1927 the economic brains and resources of America could have been marshaled to exercise a corrective influence all along the line. As time wore on, President Hoover sensed this, but his plea to stop wage cutting went unheeded.

Concerted advance action throughout the highly strategic areas of prices, taxes, and wages, accompanied by moderate public works, would have written a different story and gone a long way toward maintaining our economy in equilibrium. Much of this could have been voluntary; some would have required legislation or compulsion. Prompt public moves in a limited sphere might have averted a major economic catastrophe. There would have been no occasion for the infinitely more sweeping governmental undertakings which the actual catastrophe provoked.

This illustration suggests a variety of reasons why such a system for budgetary production and employment should simplify and pare down the governmental structure. The testing of each separate administrative institution in terms of a single American economic policy would help weed out duplication and cross purposes. A constant inventory of economic trends in general and of the economic consequences of policies already in effect would encourage the stich in time that saves nine. By keeping our economic affairs on an even keel, the proliferation of remedial and rescue ventures can be avoided. In short, to compress these analogies into a rule of thumb:

If the American Government, in concert with industry, agriculture, and labor, did a few things very well, it would become unnecessary for it to attempt under duress of emergency a great variety of things with varying degrees of success.

Of course, the economic specifics for effecting a smooth transition from war to peace are very different from those which might have averted or have minimized the depression of the thirties. But the full employment bill does not involve precommitment to details. It presents instead a new method for developing sound measures to meet current problems in their sequence. It has the merit of being opportune, without the demerit of resorting habitually to improvisation to handle a crisis. It leaves room for fresh experiment without abandoning the hard lessons of experience.

What, in truth, has our experience taught us? By way of illustration, more than half a century ago we initiated the antitrust laws. It is not important, here, to appraise whether these laws were wise or not. The point to be made is that even while Uncle Sam was shaking the big stick at the trusts, Federal tariff and tax policies moved in diametrically the opposite direction—toward encouraging nothing less than large-scale enterprise and monopoly. Not only were these two sets of policies in conflict—responsive to different social pressures and tuned to tickle different political ears—but there was never much meticulous checking as to whether they were accomplishing clear objectives, however inconsistent these might be.

Moreover, the failure to orientate the antitrust laws themselves to goals for the economy as a whole, led inescapably to vagaries when we came to apply them. We commenced to promote recovery in 1933 by a virtual suspension of these laws. We sought to prevent business recession after 1937 by reinvigorating them. And we have gone about promoting the war effort in some quarters by enforcing antitrust laws, in other quarters by ignoring them.

In contrast, the series of economic measures enacted in 1933 and after represented a concerted effort to develop a system of interrelated public policies. Nonetheless, it has been observed frequently that the National Industrial Recovery Act and the Agricultural Adjustment Act, the two big cylinders of the New Deal recovery machine, were in some degree incompatible.

There were three main programs under the Recovery Act itself—one designed to strengthen labor through encouragement of collective bargaining; another, to strengthen trade associations and tending toward restricted production; and the third, to expand production and employment through public works. These programs soon became conspicuously strange bedfellows. Some of the conflicts were smoothed over; none was completely rationalized.

Our need for a unified American economic policy is not limited to times of stress. Our social security program sprang from emergency in the midthirties, but in the years since, the program as it has developed has exhibited the same need for wider unity. Take unemployment compensation which was advocated along three lines:

To spur managements to concentrate upon stabilizing employment;

To check the spread of unemployment by maintaining purchasing power; and

To provide compensation (not charity) for those unemployed.

These three purposes are not mutually exclusive; all of them are worthwhile, but the system should delineate paramount and secondary objectives and be accompanied by some device for measuring success in achieving each of them.

Collateral effects, also, should be weighed—for example, the influence of the payroll taxes imposed by the Social Security Act upon capital investment and consequently upon unemployment itself. Further, the relation of the system to other programs with kindred purposes should be explored: for example, to other stabilizing programs, such as tax incentives or the guaranteed purchase of excess products; and to other purchasing power programs, such as public works.

This adds up to the conclusion that we can have an organic social security policy only as part of an American economic policy.

The foregoing is not critical of those who have been responsible for establishing or administering separate programs of this sort. In the absence of an all-inclusive American economic policy, it is hard to arrive at a satisfying tax policy, or social security policy, or public works policy, or labor policy, or banking policy, or foreign economic policy. One test of subsidiary objectives is to fit them into the overall objective. We cannot excel in parts until we know what the whole job is—and how we are getting along with it.

This lack of a unifying thesis in economic matters explains much bickering on the home front. It sheds light on seemingly contradictory public action, on overlapping in governmental agencies; and on the blurred line between what we need for a period of crisis and what we need for all time. Moreover, current discussion as to streamlining Congress overlooks too often that reorganization can be approached fruitfully only through prior clarification. An articulation of policies and goals would open the way for improved functioning by the Congress as a policy-making body and for the most satisfactory division of labor with the Chief Executive.

Thus the full-employment bill, as now drawn, provides for the initial development of the national production and employment budget by the President and its submission to a congressional joint committee for subsequent review and action. In view of the scope of the undertaking and the prime desirability of evoking maximum accord in testing it out, thought might be given to placing the initial development of the budget in the hands of an American economic committee, constituted by law and containing representation from both Cabinet and Congress, with a permanent staff supplemented by a rotating staff drawn from the departments concerned.

Such a plan would offer interesting possibilities for adjusting the principle of separating legislative, judicial, and executive powers, as written into the Constitution, to the increasing interplay and overlapping of congressional and Presidential functions in matters of high policy.

If an American economic committee of this type were established it might well include, also, members appointed by the President to represent industry, agriculture, labor, and consumers. The preparation of a national production and employment budget necessarily involves what free enterprise is going to do no less than what the Government is going to do. Its very essence is an appraisal of interaction between the two. Its very spirit is accord. It needs to be initiated in an atmosphere of maximum cooperation and give and take. For this reason, to bring nongovernmental representatives more explicitly into such a flexible process seems more important than to preserve rigid concepts as to the governmental structure.

It can be argued that part of the reason why pressure groups have been so unconscionably at one another's throats, why their specialized objectives often seem so far abstracted from the common good, is that they so seldom sense that good as a common goal, or have had any chance to participate in a general drive to attain it.

THE CHALLENGE OF 60 MILLION JOBS

More unity arising from more common knowledge is the essence of the full-employment bill. The measure is founded upon the proposition that nothing is worse than to contribute to the confusion of the people at large—or to make more difficult their lines of communication when major decisions in national policy are underway.

A national production and employment budget would set objectives each year based on realities, in terms understandable to everybody, and related to our common undertakings as a nation. If it did no more than that, it would bring into our public affairs a clarity, a wholesomeness, and a dignity that would strengthen immeasurably our free institutions in the years ahead.

But the full-employment bill is founded, also, on another proposition—that our American way of life and livelihood, with all its admitted imperfections, is a good one. We are committed to it by our history and our idea—and committed by the same token to remedy our imperfections as we go along. Such a course is consistent with our essential practicality and inventiveness as a people, with our emphasis on individual enterprise and our adventuresome democracy.

The human materials with which we have to deal are mostly men of good will, who know the dangers we all face unless we devise more rational ways to get rid of mass unemployment, and who know equally well the benefits we can all look for if we do. The task before us is to gather up tools in our American kit which have stood us in good stead in other great tasks and emergencies, check them against accomplishment, and improve and align them systematically for use in meeting the great test of the postwar era.

How Special Tax Provisions Get Enacted

When he wrote this article Stanley S. Surrey was a Professor at the Harvard Law School. He is now an Assistant Secretary of the Treasury.

RECENTLY THERE has been considerable criticism directed against the existence in our tax laws of provisions granting special treatment to certain groups or individuals. The purpose of this article is to consider the question of why the Congress enacts these special tax provisions.

SOME MAJOR FACTORS

High Rates of Tax • The high rates of the individual income tax, and of the estate and gift taxes, are probably the major factor in producing special tax legislation. This is, in a sense, a truism, for without something to be relieved of, there would be no need to press for relief. The point is that the average congressman does not basically believe in the present rates of income tax in the upper brackets. When he sees them applied to individual cases, he thinks them too high and therefore unfair. Any argument for relief which starts off by stating that these high rates are working a "special hardship" in a particular case or are "penalizing" a particular taxpayer—to use some words from the tax lobbyist's approved list of effective phrases—has the initial advantage of having a sympathetic listener.

Tax Polarity • The existence of two rate structures in the income tax and of two types of taxes on the transfer of wealth permits a congressman to favor a special group by placing its situation under the lower rate structure or the less effective tax. Thus, the presence of the twenty-five-per-cent capital-gains rate enables Congress to shift an executive stock option from the high rates applying to executive compensation to the lower capital-gains rate. If there were no special capital-gains rate, or if we did not tax capital gains at all, this shift could not be made, since a congressman would not completely exempt the stock option. Similarly, the presence of a gift tax permits certain transfers of wealth, such as transferred life insurance, to be shifted from the higher estate tax to the lower gift tax. As a consequence, given this congressional tendency, we reach the paradox that having a gift tax as well as an estate tax may, given the present lack of proper co-ordination of the two taxes, result in less effective taxation of certain transfers of wealth than if we relied only on an estate tax.

Technical Complexity • The high rates of tax, the complexities of modern business, the desires of the wealthy and middle-income groups for clear tax charts to guide their family planning, the Government's need for protection against tax avoidance, the claims of tax equity, and various other factors have combined to make the income, estate, and gift taxes exceedingly complex in technical detail. These technicalities involve the drawing of countless dividing lines. Consequently, a case on the high-tax side of a line may closely resemble the cases on the other side receiving more favorable tax treatment. The result is a fertile ground for assertions of inequity and hardship as particular taxpayers desire legislation to bend the dividing lines and thereby extend the favorable treatment to their situations. Also, faulty tax planning, ill-advised legal steps, or transactions concluded in ignorance of tax law can produce severe tax consequences. These "tax penalties" could have been averted under an informed tax guidance that would have taken the taxpayer safely through the technical tax maze. In these circumstances, the taxpayer facing severe monetary hurt because of a "mere technicality" (to use the phrase that will be pressed on the congressman) is quite likely to evoke considerable sympathy for his plight.

History and Politics • The accidents of tax history also play a major role in the existence of special provisions. Tax-exempt securities in large part achieved their favored status through the vagaries of constitutional interpretation and not through any special desire to relieve the wealthy. Percentage depletion for oil and gas and the deduction of intangible drilling expenses have their roots in legislative compromises and administrative interpretation which for the most part do not appear to have been

planned as special-interest relief. It is only later that the extent
of the tax generosity inherent in such provisions is comprehended.
But by then they are in the law, the problem of the group benefited is one of defense rather than attack, and the strategic advantages are all with that group. This is especially so when the area
involved touches on major political matters, as in the case of
percentage depletion and tax-exempt securities.

Political considerations naturally overhang this whole area, for
taxation is a sensitive and volatile matter. Any major congressional action represents the compromises of the legislator as he
weighs and balances the strong forces constantly focused on him
by the pressure groups of the country. Many special provisions
—capital gains, for one—are caught in these swirling pressures.

*Separation of Executive and Legislative Branches of Govern-
ment* • But many of the tax provisions we are considering do not
lie at this political level. They are simply a part of the technical
tax law. They are not of major importance in their revenue impact. But they are of major importance to the group or individual
benefited and they are glaring in their departure from tax fairness. The inquiry, therefore, must here be directed toward some
of the institutional features in the tax-legislation process which
may be responsible for special provisions of this technical variety.

Congress occupies the role of mediator between the tax views
of the executive and the demands of the pressure groups. This is
so whether the tax issue involved is a major political matter or a
minor technical point. The Congress is zealous in maintaining this
position in the tax field.

The Congress regards the shaping of a revenue bill as very
much its prerogative. It will seek the views of the executive, for
there is a respect for the sustained labors of those in the executive
departments and also a recognition, varying with the times, of
the importance of presidential programs. But control over the
legislation itself, both as to broad policies and as to details, rests
with the Congress. Hence a congressman, and especially a member of the tax comittees, is in a position to make the tax laws bend
in favor of a particular individual or group despite strong objection from the executive branch. Under such a governmental system the importance to the tax structure of the institutional factors
that influence a congressman's decision is obvious.

SOME INSTITUTIONAL FACTORS

The Congressman's Desire To Be Helpful • A congressman's instincts are to be helpful and friendly. If it were otherwise, he would not be in Congress. When a constituent, or some other person who is in a position to claim attention, seeks legislative action, the congressman likes to respond within reason. If the proposal presented to him is at all rational he will, in all probability, at least introduce it in bill form so as not to offend the constituent. If the congressman is not a member of one of the tax committees, that may end the matter—but it may not, for the proposal has been launched and lies ready to be pushed ahead by whatever pressures may be generated in its behalf.

Lack of Congressional Appreciation of Departure From Fairness • In many cases the congressman considering a special tax provision may not realize that tax fairness is at all involved. He sees only the problem of the particular constituent or group concerned. The case in this focus may be very appealing, for human beings are involved with human problems. The income tax, always an impersonal, severe, monetary burden, becomes an oppressive force bearing down on men in difficulty. The congressman may therefore not even appreciate that arguments of over-all fairness and equity have any relation to the question, or may very well think them too intangible and remote. Provisions for the relief of the blind and the aged are perhaps illustrations. Or the congressman, moved simply by a desire to help a constituent, may not understand the ramifications of the proposal. He is not a tax technician and he may view the proposal in isolation rather than perceive its relationship to the intricate technical structure of the revenue code. The proposal, so viewed, becomes merely a "little old amendment" which helps a constituent and does no harm. His brother congressmen are quite willing to be good fellows and go along, especially if the congressman urging the proposal is well-liked. After all, they too from time to time will have "little old amendments" to propose. Thus, in 1955 the Ways and Means Committee decided that in the initial consideration of members' bills dealing with technical matters it would allow each member one bill to be considered and then reported by the full committee if the bill met with unanimous agreement.

The Treasury Department's Presentation • The congressman's failure to recognize that tax fairness is at all involved may often be due to the inadequacy of the Treasury Department's presentation of the issues. This is not said critically, but by way of explanation. The problem facing the Treasury in these matters is formidable. The interested constituents or groups are generally skillful in presenting their cases in appealing form. Their energies are concentrated on one matter; they have time and money to devote to it; they may have the advantage of personal acquaintance, directly or through intermediaries, with the congressman; they can obtain skilled counsel informed on the ways of the Congress. The Treasury's tax staff must tackle all of these problems; its members are usually not chosen for skill in the presentation of issues or in handling congressmen; although on the whole remarkably good, considering the compensation, they are rarely among the ablest in the tax field, nor do they usually have the needed experience.

Lack of Omniscience on the Part of the Treasury • The treasury tax staff is not omniscient. Yet understanding approaching omniscience is needed to do its job. A lack of knowledge on any particular matter, a failure of skill at any moment, can be fatal. The approach of the average congressman is to hear the private group, find out in general what it wants, react sympathetically for a variety of reasons, and then ask the Treasury whether there is any objection to the proposal. If the Treasury is off its guard and acquiesces, the proposal becomes law. If the Treasury is unprepared and presents a weak case, the proposal becomes law. Equally serious is the in-between situation in which the Treasury acknowledges that some hardship is present in the particular situation, but points out that the difficulty is but a phase of a general problem and that it has not yet been able fully to analyze the general area. It therefore urges that the particular proposal be postponed until further study is given to the whole matter. But recognition of some hardship and of some merit in his particular proposal is all that the congressman needs. His constituent wants relief from that admitted hardship now, and not years later when the whole matter has been thought through and his case fitted into a solution appropriate for many cases. Hence the con-congressman will seek approval of the proposal in the limited form necessary to solve the particular problem presented to him —and a special tax provision is thereby born.

Lack of Opposition Apart From the Treasury Department to Proponents of Special Tax Provisions • The critical importance that attaches to the level of treasury competence and the fatal consequences of any slip on its part derive from its unique position in tax legislation. The question, "Who speaks for tax equity and tax fairness?," is answered today largely in terms of only the Treasury Department. If that department fails to respond, then tax fairness has no champion before the Congress. Moreover, it must respond with vigor and determination, and after a full explanation of the matter it must take a forthright stand on the issues. A Treasury Department that contents itself with explaining the issues and then solemnly declaring the matter to be one for the policy determination of Congress abdicates its responsibility. The congressman understands aggressiveness and a firm position. He is often in the position of the small boy inwardly seeking parental bounds for his conduct while outwardly declaiming against them. He may not accept policy guidance from the treasury policy spokesman, but he wants it presented. He will invariably interpret a treasury statement that the matter is one for his own policy decision as a victory for the seeker of the special provision.

Thus, in the tax bouts that a congressman witnesses the Treasury is invariably in one corner of the ring. Assuming the Treasury decides to do battle, which is hardly a safe assumption at all times, it is the Treasury versus percentage depletion, the Treasury versus capital gains, the Treasury versus this constituent, the Treasury versus that private group. The effect on the congressman as referee is inevitable. He simply cannot let every battle be won by the Treasury, and hence every so often he gives the victory to the sponsors of a special provision. Moreover, the Treasury is not an impersonal antagonist—it is represented before the Congress by individuals. These individuals are constantly forced to say that enactment of this proposal will be unfair, and the same of the next, and the next. The congressman, being only human, is bound from time to time to look upon these individuals as the Cassandras of the tax world. To avoid this dilemma, the Treasury in a close case will sometimes concede the issue if the proposal can be narrowly confined. It feels compelled to say "yes" once in a while simply to demonstrate that it maintains a balanced judgment and posses a sense of fairness. A special provision is thus enacted simply because it happens to have somewhat more merit than the numerous other special proposals before the committees and because an affirmative answer here by the Treasury will protect negative responses to the other proposals.

The Congressional Tax Staff • The description of the Treasury as the principal and often the sole defender of tax fairness calls for a consideration of the role of the congressional tax staff. Most of the congressional tax technicians are members of the staff of the Joint Committee on Internal Revenue Taxation and as such serve both the House Ways and Means Committee and the Senate Finance Committee. There are a few technicians attached to the separate committees, and the clerks of the committees can play a very important role if they are personally so inclined. But institutionally the chief guidance given to Congress by its own employees comes from this joint committee staff.

The members of this staff work closely with the treasury tax technicians. Their work on the details of proposals and drafts is highly important, but the task of policy formulation and policy guidance to the congressmen appears to be reserved exclusively to the chief of that staff. His role is a difficult and unenviable one. Many congressmen pass along to him the tax proposals that they are constantly receiving from their constituents. Undoubtedly, the Chief of Staff discreetly but effectively blocks many of these proposals from proceeding further. But he also, whatever his inclinations may be, cannot in his situation always say "no." Perhaps inevitably on the crucial issues his role tends to be that of the advocate of the congressman advancing a particular proposal on behalf of a special group. The special-interest groups cannot appear in the executive sessions of the committees, and the congressman sympathetic to their point of view is not technically equipped to present their case; he tends to look to the Chief of Staff to assume that task. Further, he looks to the Chief of Staff to formulate the technical compromises which will resolve the dispute between the special-interest group and the Treasury. The Chief of Staff must therefore work closely with the congressmen and be "brilliantly sensitive to their views." He must necessarily be able to gauge the degree of interest that a congressman may have in a proposal and weigh that in the consideration of the guidance he will give.

Because of these institutional pressures the Chief of Staff is very often the opponent of the Treasury Department before the tax committees. As a result, the difficulties for the average congressman on the tax committees become even greater. The issues get more and more complex as the "experts" disagree, and the congressman can hardly follow the technical exchanges. He is quite often content to fall back on the comfortable thought that, since the congressional expert appears to disagree with the treasury experts, there is adequate technical justification for voting either way. Hence the congressman is free to be guided by his own sympathies and instincts. Since generally these sympathies are in favor of the private groups, their proposals obtain his vote.

Unfortunately agreement between the congressional Chief of Staff and the Treasury can sometimes present just as difficult a problem. When the two disagree, at least the congressman who is seeking to discover the real issues may find them exposed at some time through this disagreement of experts. But if the experts agree, the effect is often to foreclose any real committee consideration of the issues. The congressman may be lulled into thinking that no significant issues are involved, and the proposal therefore becomes law. But if the government experts have erred, or if they have incorrectly gauged the congressional sentiment, special benefits may well result which the congressman would not have sanctioned had he understood what was involved.

Lack of Effective Aid From the Tax Bar • The lack of any pressure-group allies for the Treasury in its representation of the tax-paying public could have been remedied in part by effective aid from the tax bar. Yet for a good many years the vocal tax bar not only withheld any aid but very often conducted itself as an ally of the special pressure groups. Many a lawyer representing a client seeking a special provision could without much difficulty obtain American Bar Association or local-bar-association endorsement for his proposal. He could then appear before Congress and solemnly exhibit the blessing of the legal profession. In fact, the activity of the Bar Association in this respect became so obvious that it seemingly boomeranged—many a congressman began instinctively to smell mischief when presented with a Bar Association tax proposal or endorsement.

Lack of Public Knowledge of Special Tax Provisions • Perhaps the most significant aspect of the consideration of special tax provisions by the Congress is that it usually takes place without any awareness of these events by the general public. Almost entirely, these matters lie outside of the public's gaze, outside of the voter's knowledge. The special provisions which are enacted lie protected in the mysterious complex statutory jargon of the tax law. This technical curtain is impenetrable to the newspapers and other information media. The public hears of debate over tax reduction or tax increase and it may learn something about the general rate structure. But it seldom learns that the high rates have no applicability to much of the income of certain wealthy groups. Nor does it understand how this special taxpayer or that special group is relieved of a good part of its tax burden. All of these matters are largely fought out behind this technical curtain. Hence the congressman favoring these special provisions has for the most part no accounting to make to the voters for his action. He is thereby much freer to lend a helping hand here and there to a group which has won his sympathy or which is pressing him for results.

The Relationship of Special Tax Provisions to Private-Relief Bills • Some of these special provisions represent simply private-relief claims for the particular individual benefited. While phrased as amendments to the tax law, they are only money claims against the Government based on the equities asserted to exist. Thus, it is said of a senator skilled in congressional ways that he would ask the legislative draftsman preparing the draft of a particular tax provision to make the amendment as general in language and as specific in application as was possible. The tax committees and the Treasury have not solved the problem of how to handle these special bills. Curiously enough, some tax situations do come through the judiciary committees as private-relief bills along with other private-relief bills involving claims against the Government. These bills may involve, for example, a removal of the barrier of the statute of limitations in cases thought equitable, or the recovery of funds spent for revenue stamps lost in some fashion.

Here they are subject to the criteria developed over the decades by those committees in the handling of private-claims bills. These criteria are reasonably strict, and few of the bills pass the Congress. Of those that do succeed, a number are vetoed, and a veto is customarily regarded as a final disposition of the bill.

Many situations come before the tax committees that are quite comparable, in that the tax proposal is equivalent to a money claim against the Government, equal to the tax to be saved, sought for a specific taxpayer on equitable grounds. This is especially true in the case of proposals of a retroactive character. In the tax committees these special proposals tend to take on the coloration of an amendment to the tax code of the same character as all the various substantive tax matters before these committees. In essence, all amendments to the tax laws that private groups push on their own behalf are designed to lower taxes for the proponents and thereby relieve them from a tax burden to which they are subject. The special proposals thus become simply one more amendment in the long list of changes to be considered. The proponents of these special proposals are thereby able to cloak the fact that they are presenting private-relief claims against the Government. This is especially so when the proposal is considered as merely one more item in a general revenue bill. Here it is also protected from the threat—and fate—of a presidential veto. Even when the proposal is considered as a separate bill, the fact that it is merely one of the bills before a tax committee that is considering a great many substantive bills involving amendments to the tax code generally produces the same result. The committee will tend to focus on the proposal as curing a substantive defect in the law and lose sight of the fact that the special proposal is essentially a private-relief bill.

The Patent System in Action

WALTON HAMILTON

The late Walton Hamilton was an economist at the Yale Law School and a practicing lawyer in Washington, D.C.

SPEECH AS CERTAINLY as kitchen middens tells its story of activity. The patent system in action, as distinguished from the patent statutes, has left its deposit in the American language. The word-hoard which it has created speaks as accurately and as eloquently as do the documents themselves. Note, for example, the term trap patent, that is, a patent taken out, or at least applied for, not primarily to secure a grant but in the expectation of drawing into the open all fruitful research within the orbit of invention. Applications for patents are confidential and not matters of public record; but if there are two or more applications for exclusive rights to the same invention, or if there is a serious overlap between the two, the Patent Office declares an interference and an adversary proceeding is staged. A line of publicity about the filing inspired by the applicant, or even a rumor, may be enough to convey the caution that other inventors operating in the area had better get their applications in. The applicant is always at liberty to allege inadvertence and amend; and as knowledge comes to him, he can rewrite to enlarge his claims in terms of what others have done.

Then there is the umbrella patent, a thing which is exactly what its name implies, a grant written so broadly as to cover all future innovation within its ambit. The dragnet patent is again a self-explanatory term and very much of a kind with the umbrella patent. It connotes a grant so comprehensive in its sweep and so closely fashioned in detail that any impending invention will be caught up and sterilized in its finely meshed net.

The blocking patent is a patent upon an essential step in the development of a technology. An exclusive right at a strategic point is used to block advances which others might make in the art. A series of fencing patents—note the plural—may be used to fence in and thus to protect the technology of a corporation against attack by its competitors. It is economic armament for the defense of the industrial imperium. But it invites offensive as well as defensive use. An executive has testified that it is the policy of his corporation to make, and take out patents upon, improvements on the technical processes of its rivals. If in this way all roads are blocked, the industrial processes of the competitor are fenced in against advance. The competitor is confined to methods of production which, with the advance of the arts, become more and more out of date.

A chain patent, or more accurately a chain of patents, represents a kind of ultimate in aspiration. Chains may be horizontal, stretching through letter patent [1] after letter patent in a huge portfolio, or the chain may be vertical. If a useful art takes a progressive course, its mutations become subject to the grant of patents. As patents expire and pass into the public domain, they are available to all comers, but the forward steps in the industry are still subject to private control and the newcomer is likely to discover that he has access to no more than an obsolete technology. He is quite free to enter the business and to market his wares, but the cost of methods which are no longer up to date may hinder, and the quality of the product may not meet current standards.

In general, where technologies are once subjected to private government in their active form, the chances run strongly against their return to the public domain. A mere glance at this catalogue of terms makes it clear that the word list is not that of scientists and inventors, but of business executives and their attorneys. The list itself testifies that in the patent grant there is a flexible and multitask instrument of private government.

It is out of the question here to set down in classic style a disquisition upon the letter patent as a political sanction, or to explore the many distinct ways in which it has been employed by corporations in establishing and maintaining systems of private government. A docket of some three cases will be enough, not to show the diversity which exists, but to indicate that there is diversity.

A very simple case is that of a sulfa derivative. The original

1. ["Letter patent" is simply the legal term for the written document issued by the government which confers upon the person applying for a patent the exclusive right (for a limited time) to make, sell, and use his invention. *Editor.*]

product came into use as a dye and the patent had expired before its therapeutic character was discovered. Its employment as
a medicine gave promise of a substantial market, and the manufacturing drug houses were easily persuaded to make and vend
the commodity. The stumbling block was that, with an unpat-
ented drug, the houses could not assure themselves and their outlets of the margins of profit to which they had become accustomed.
A way out was to improve the product, and from the simple base
a number of variants were derived. One ethical drug house had
contrived the formula and was filing with the Patent Office its
application for a grant. A second house had moved along the
same line, and hearing the rumors in the trade, made contact with
the first. In a short time, two other manufacturers, both of whom
had done some experimental work, asked to be included in the
accord. In the end some nine companies came into the picture.
All proved to be of so pacific a nature that they deemed it best to
settle their conflicting claims by a gentlemen's agreement rather
than by resort to law.

So the issue as to which one had priority and therefore was
entitled to the patent was brushed aside as of no consequence.
It was agreed that only one application for a patent was to be
made, and the choice of the company was left not to technicians
but to the attorneys. Thus the Patent Office, unconfused by a
multiplex of applications, had no difficulty in recognizing and
rewarding the sole and true inventor. It was agreed that the party
to which the patent should issue was to license each of the other
eight to make and vend the product. In this instance it would
have been easy for any one of the eight houses to go into production, to invite a suit for infringement, and in the end to break
the patent. It is obvious that what each of them was after was not
access to technology—that was to be had for nothing—but something else, and that something else was a sanction for a concert of
action in the fixing of prices. To any charge that prices were made
by agreement, it could be pleaded in defense that the patent
owner was doing no more than giving effect to the exclusive right
with which he had been endowed by the Government.

A different case of industrial government is that of vitamin D.
Who it was who discovered or invented or at least contrived the
process for the synthetic production of vitamin D we do not
know. We know the names of the experimenters, a great deal

about the work they did, the material which appeared in the learned periodicals, and especially the frantic search by ethical drug houses for inventors in whose names claims might be presented. But a study of the voluminous testimony gives no claimant identity to the sole and true inventor. However, the dominant patent was taken out in the name of a professor at the University of Wisconsin, and was assigned to the Wisconsin Alumni Research Foundation. The interest of the Foundation was not in using the letter patent as an instrument of industrial government. It was rather to secure from it the maximum of revenue for its research work. To this end attorneys skilled in the practical art of turning letters patent to account were consulted.

As a result, the Foundation was able to put into operation an ingenious scheme of exclusive licenses. A license conferred upon an Illinois corporation the exclusive right to employ the process in the manufacture of cooked breakfast foods. A second license conferred upon another corporation a like right with respect to uncooked breakfast foods. A third conferred a similar privilege in respect to foods for horses, asses, and mules. Two licenses, each exclusive in character, were made to cover dairy herds, the one for cows whose milk was destined for fluid use, the other for cows whose milk was intended to enter manufactured milk products. A separate license was given in respect to food for dogs, foxes, and wolves; another for food intended for feline consumption. There were two licenses in respect to food for mice, the one for mice kept as pets, the other for those dedicated to the service of science in the laboratory.

Thus the licenses were all shaped in accordance with the distinct uses to which various food products were put, and the rate of royalties was neatly adjusted to the circumstances of each particular case. By such nice gradation the maximum yield was substantially in excess of what it would have been had the rule of a single price for a single commodity been strictly observed. The end result lay beyond the intention of the Foundation. A single firm in each of the several fields, by the virtue of the exclusive license, was given a competitive advantage. The private government inherent in the license system set in motion a trend toward monopoly throughout a vital segment of the economy.

For a number of years this scheme operated like clockwork. Eventually it failed not from its own weight, but because it became a victim of legal hazards. The Foundation rather unwisely instituted suits for infringement, and in one of these a sentence of invalidity was bestowed upon the patent. In the end the scheme fell because the courts refused to recognize the sanction upon which it was built. It came into being, flourished like the green bay tree, and passed into oblivion.

The third and classic example is the case of Hartford Empire. The industry of glass containers, like many others, came into being under the rule of competition. Production was a matter of handicraft, demanding of the key workers a skill in the art of blowing. The investment required to operate a factory was modest. The raw materials were plentiful and easy of access. The number of firms was quite large. In time, machine technology came into the industry and two distinct processes for turning out glass containers were invented, the one built around the general idea of blowing, the other, that of molding. The machines did not demand an excessive amount of capital, and the technology embodied in them was, for all of their complicated appearance, quite simple.

The operation of the process imposed no excessive demand for know-how. The resulting situation was much like that in bituminous coal. Competition easily became excessive and even destructive; and, as in coal, some preventive seemed to be necessary if a flood of bankruptcies was to be avoided. The pattern of the industry was not the kind which invited the regulatory hand of the Government. If there was to be order, solvency, and salvation, it was up to the firms within it to work out their own destiny.

In time it became evident to the dominant firms that some sort of get-together was needed. How wide was the therapeutic search, and how many alternatives were considered, we do not know. In the end it was determined to set up a new corporation, not as a producer of glass containers, but as an overlord to the firms in the trade. If such things as order, a neat structure for the industry, an elimination of excess capacity, and a stable market were to be had, there would have to be some compulsion. If the overlord was to compel, he would have to have sanctions with which to authenticate its mandates. It was decided, therefore, that all letters patent which together covered virtually the whole of the machine technology should be transferred from the several firms to the newly created Hartford Empire Company. The firms were to become the licensees of Hartford Empire, and the licenses were to be made the instruments through which the commands of the overlord were to be imposed upon them.

Upon these premises there was established a clean-cut and articulate private government. The license agreement together with the regulations, through which it was given effect, constituted the law of the industry. From headquarters at Hartford, the seat of the Empire, lines of authority went out to all accredited manufacturers. If its mandates were not obeyed, there was first a warning. On a second act of disobedience, the offender might be put on probation, and for the third he was subject to exclusion from the industry. Here, if the corporate police system proved inadequate, it might be supplemented by an appeal to outside authority. The Hartford license conferred upon its recipient a limited and specified right to make use of the technology covered by the arsenal of patents, upon terms and conditions enumerated. If the license holder overstepped the limits or violated any of the terms or conditions, he became subject to an action in court for patent infringement. By this device the courts of the United States might be invoked to police the private government of the industry.

The first task of Hartford Empire was to wield scattered and conglomerate firms into an orderly whole. The stronger firms were without question given licenses. The weaker firms were compelled to accept licenses upon terms dictated by Hartford Empire or else face suit for patent infringement. As order was brought out of miscellany, the number of firms was substantially reduced with a corresponding increase in size. Each firm was free to accept or refuse the accord, but if it stayed out, it did so at its peril. Here a cardinal principle of administration was employed—compulsions must be disguised as choices.

The concrete detail of the private government was not neglected. Any person content to use obsolete methods was free to enter the industry and to take the consequences of his rash action. But if he wanted to use up-to-date technology and to become a real competitor, he had to seek a license from Hartford Empire. His application was referred to the committee on character, and this committee was there to see to it that only persons of the highest integrity were permitted to become manufacturers of glass containers. A criterion of such integrity is the candidate's standing in the community, and that standing is not unassociated with financial resources. In addition to the wherewithal, the newcomer was not welcomed unless there was a place for him in the industry. If the market for any ware was already adequately supplied, it was evident that there was no place for the applicant. The old firms, as well as such new ones as might be admitted, had to live up to the law of the industry.

Order required that each member have its fixed and appointed domain, and this was effected by the provisions written into the separate licenses. Thus, one concern was licensed to manufacture whiskey bottles only; another had as its domain beer bottles; and one concern was free to manufacture beer bottles so long as they were amber in color. One concern was licensed to manufacture wine bottles; another in this area was limited to wine bottles for sacramental use only. More than one concern was licensed to manufacture milk bottles, but their territorial domains were kept apart. One concern was licensed to manufacture fruit jars and paid royalties to Hartford Empire for the privilege. The anomaly is that the firm used a distinct process covered by letters patent of its own and made no use of the technology of Hartford Empire.

As with the distinct fields in which members of the industry were permitted to operate, so there was a geographical division of territories. So, too, quotas were assigned to the various firms in order to insure that the market for any particular kind of glass container should not become glutted. And the prices which the various licensees were to charge were themselves fixed by the overlord. Hartford Empire, of course, had access to the books and accounts of all the firms, was at all times fully informed about the business of each, and was constantly vigilant in its supervisory office.

How neat and orderly the whole system was is made evident in a colloquy at a public hearing between an attorney for the Department of Justice and the general counsel for the Empire. The Government lawyer inquired if the attorney for the company was familiar with the case of *New State Ice Company v. Liebman*, a case in which the United States Supreme Court held that the sovereign state of Oklahoma lacked authority to impose a detailed pattern of regulation upon its ice industry. The company attorney expressed thorough familiarity with the case. He was then asked if the Empire was not regulating, even regimenting, the glass container industry in greater detail and with more thoroughness than Oklahoma had attempted. His answer was simply that we do these things so much better than the state of Oklahoma.

A Federal antitrust suit resulted in a decree modifying, if not outlawing, a number of the practices of the company. In the public records there is little to tell of what has happened since the judgment, but it is well known that agencies of government relax their vigilance once a case is closed. It is hard to believe that the attorneys, whose skills found expression in the creation of the Empire, have not been able to rise to the emergency.

The Political Impasse in Farm Support Legislation

THE EDITORS OF THE YALE LAW JOURNAL

This originally appeared as an unsigned article in the *Yale Law Journal*. The editors of the Journal acknowledged their debt to Professor Robert Salisbury of Washington University for permission to draw on his research.

To ALLEVIATE the severe depression in agriculture during the 1930's, Congress passed the Agricultural Adjustment Acts. Although the emergency of the thirties has long passed, the approach of that emergency legislation still forms the basis of our laws. Now, as then, the government undertakes to control supplies and to support prices at "parity" levels. If the producers of designated crops, called "basic" crops, agree to restrict the number of acres in production, they become eligible to receive government loans secured by the crops they produce. The amount loaned per bushel or pound of production is determined by the percent of "parity" established by law. A full, or 100 percent of parity price would give agricultural commodities a purchasing power with respect to articles that farmers buy, equivalent to the purchasing power of agricultural commodities in an earlier period, designated to serve as a standard of normalcy. Theoretically, the acreage restrictions should so reduce supply that market prices would rise above the percent of parity loaned, causing farmers to pay off their loans and sell their crops. Since the loans are secured only by the crops themselves, if the supply did not decrease, or the demand increase, sufficiently to raise the market price above the loan level, farmers would choose to keep the greater loan amounts, and let the government foreclose on the crops. The consequent removal of a part of the supply from the market into government storage, would work to increase the market price— hopefully, above the loan levels so that the government would stop accumulating supplies. Thus, theoretically, the programs would work to even out fluctuations in supply, and to "support" prices by balancing supply with demand at the specified percent of a parity price. However, economic changes, especially technological innovations in agricultural production, have made these supports and controls even less effective. Over the long run, supplies have not been reduced, prices have remained below the support-loan levels set by law, and the government has accumulated tremendous quantities of the supported crops. There are now nearly nine billion dollars worth of agricultural commodities stockpiled, the storage of which alone costs the government over one and one-half million dollars per day. Virtually no one likes these results. Since there has been such full discussion of the disadvantages of the programs in both popular and scholarly publications, little would be gained by further detailing here the standard outrages and the commonplace enormities. The difficult question is: given the undesirability of the present situation, what can, in fact, be done about it?

There is considerable agreement on many broad, long-range objectives. But there is general disagreement as to how these goals should be implemented. Candidates and administrations, universities and farm organizations turn out one "solution" after another. Although many may be economically sound, none has been adopted by Congress.

Conflicts among various political interest groups have prevented innovation in farm policy. Therefore, meaningful debate about possible solutions requires an understanding of the limitations imposed by the realities of politics. This article will describe the political interest groups active in the area of farm price-support legislation, and explain why and where the conflicts among them arise. Next, it will examine the effects of these political factors on the fate of a few of the more important recent proposals.

THE POLITICAL CONTEXT

Classically defined, a political interest or interest group is men, formally organized or not, who desire to obtain advantages through government, and who thereby come into conflict with other men. Conflict results either because the same advantage is desired by both groups, and is scarce, or because the second group would be at a relative disadvantage if the first group obtained its desires. This definition emphasizes groups because an individual cannot generally be a significant factor in governmental politics unless other individuals join with him. It requires no formal organization of groups because even unorganized groups can be effective political forces. And it uses the terms interest and interest group interchangeably because the present existence of a group is not required, but only the present existence of a common interest which could become an effective political force if that interest became the subject of political controversy.

Since agricultural price-support laws are a form of economic regulation, the groups concerned with them are usually based on economic interests. Rational, objective economic self-interest is not the sole determinant of political behavior; such behavior reflects the totality of the experiences of each of the participants. For example, a strong commitment to individualism rooted in religious beliefs may lead a farmer to place a higher value on goals other than maximum economic advantage, or may even shape his perception of the direction in which his economic interests lie. It is generally true, however, that farmers align themselves in accordance with identifiable economic interests and make political demands which would advance those interests. Consequently, it is important to determine what those patterns of alliance and conflict are.

INTER-CROP CONFLICTS

Competing Crops • Where different crops compete for the same market, conflict may occur. To the extent a law benefits one crop, it puts the others at a competitive disadvantage. There are two major conflicts of this type. Since soybeans, corn, cottonseeds, dairy fats, and lard from meat animals are alternative sources for many fats, oils and shortenings, bills which benefit producers of one meet opposition from producers of the others. Likewise, corn interests oppose bills which would make wheat competitive with corn as a source of feed. At present, artificially high wheat prices maintained by the government preclude this use.

Supplier-Consumer Relation • Where some crops are consumed in the production of other agricultural commodities and the consumers do not themselves produce substantial amounts of these crops, their interest will conflict with the suppliers' interest. Livestock producers generally oppose any program which would increase their costs by raising feed grain prices. Since the demand for any given meat is highly elastic, livestock men believe they cannot increase prices to cover the increased feed costs without substantially reducing their sales. But there are some exceptions. Where farmers raising livestock also grow feed grains, they are less likely to oppose grain supports. Hog and dairy farmers fall into this category. Similarly, where the demand for livestock products is highly inelastic as in the case of fluid milk, these producers have less to fear from increased costs because they can raise prices with little effect on sales. And where periods of gestation and maturation differ among livestock, producers of animals with short periods such as hogs may be more fearful of lower feed prices than producers of animals with longer periods such as cattle. Since this difference in gestation and maturation periods causes the cattle market to respond more slowly than the hog market to an increase in grain supplies, hog producers have a more immediate fear that their own market will be glutted.

"Diverted Acres" • Even where two crops do not compete for the same markets, government programs favoring one may have a detrimental effect on the other. When acreage allotments are placed on a crop to reduce its supply and raise its price, the acres diverted from the production of that crop may be used to grow another. The increased supply of this second crop will depress its price, injuring those who had been producing it. When acreage controls were imposed on cotton and wheat producers, many of them diverted some of their acres into production of feed grain, increasing its supply and decreasing its price. Since climate, terrain, legal impediments, or the lack of expertise and capital may make it difficult for old feed grain producers to compensate for their decreased income by going into production of other crops, they opposed these controls. The use of diverted acres could create conflicts between a large number of crops which might be controlled, and a large number of other crops which might be grown in their place.

Agricultural Budget Allocation • Further conflicts may develop in the process of allocating the agricultural budget among different crops. Since the amount of funds that can be secured for price support programs is limited, and especially since legislators have perceived this to be the case, all crops may compete among themselves to maximize their individual shares of the available funds.

INTRA-CROP CONFLICTS

New Areas v. Old Areas • When it becomes profitable to produce a crop in a new area, the interests of those who historically have grown the crop may conflict with the interests of the new producers. This conflict has occurred in both cotton and wheat. In an attempt to raise cotton prices, Congress restricted cotton acreage during the 1930's. Growing privileges were allotted to individual farms on the basis of what the land had produced on the average in several prior years. During World War II Congress dropped these restrictions. Increased wartime demand combined with technological innovations to stimulate new cotton production in the western states. Since the war, the old cotton South has attempted to stem this movement by supporting reinstatement of high support programs with acreage restrictions based on past production. This interest collides with that of the new producers. The latter group desires freedom to expand production. Since they can grow cotton more efficiently, lower prices have less impact on their profit margins. Moreover, lower prices may allow these growers to expand sales in foreign markets and even to capture the domestic markets of the old growers by driving them out of business.

Similarly, old wheat producers have sought to limit new sources of wheat. Government programs have raised wheat prices to attractive levels. Although these programs include history-based production restrictions, many Corn Belt farmers with no history of wheat production have been able to take advantage of the guaranteed, high wheat prices because the law has permitted any farmer to grow at least fifteen acres. Since this exemption has benefitted these new wheat producers but has hurt old producers by glutting their market, the exemption has become the subject of political controversy.

Proximity to Markets • When commodities are perishable, and historically have been produced near consumers, differences in proximity to markets provide another basis for conflict among producers. Farmers near markets argue for controls which will insulate their historical markets from more distant suppliers. But to the extent technological innovations allow the more distant suppliers to sell profitably in these markets, they oppose such controls. This conflict has been especially intense in the determination of so-called "milkshed" areas surrounding large milk-consuming centers.

Competing Varieties and Grades • As with different crops, different varieties and grades of the same crop which compete for the same markets may conflict over programs which would give one a competitive advantage over others. This conflict occurs only where the differing varieties cannot be grown on the same land; otherwise disadvantaged producers could switch to the favored variety. Arguing that their particular variety was not in surplus, but that in fact their crop's special attributes caused more demand for it than could be filled under existing acreage restrictions, producers of certain types of wheat have secured special, more favored treatment in wheat legislation. Growers of other, more abundant varieties opposed such treatment because buyers who were unable to get enough of the preferred variety of wheat had been buying the more abundant variety as a substitute. Similarly, in seeking to have parity computed with long-staple cotton as the base, the newer, long-staple cotton producers seek advantages over the older, short-staple producers. Since in free markets the higher quality long-staple cotton would bring higher prices, and since relative price differences among varieties are maintained under the parity system, this method of computing parity accords all cotton relatively low prices, a goal sought by the newer, more efficient, long-staple, western growers and resisted by the older, less efficient, short-staple, eastern growers.

THE INVERSE

Where none of the conditions previously discussed are met, conflicts are not likely to occur. Tobacco price support programs, for example, have not engendered inter-crop conflicts. Since no other crop can be used as a substitute for tobacco, there is no inter-crop competition. Tobacco is not consumed in the production of other agricultural commodities. There have been relatively few acres diverted from tobacco to other crops as a result of acreage controls. Since small decreases in tobacco supplies increase prices significantly, tobacco programs have required little government subsidy, decreasing the likelihood of conflicts over budget allocation. Moreover, there has been little conflict *within* tobacco. Different varieties of tobacco do not compete; they each have distinct uses. Since each variety can be grown in only a few well-defined areas, these areas are substantially immune from competition from any new areas. Moreover, differences in proximity to markets are not crucial in tobacco. Therefore, each of the reasons for conflict enumerated above is not present in tobacco, and the tobacco programs have, in fact, proved particularly non-controversial in Congress.

POLITICAL VARIABLES

The shape that these inter-crop and intra-crop economic conflicts take in Congress may be conditioned by other, political factors. Some crops have superior access to key points in the legislative process. For instance, the Chairmen of the House and Senate Agriculture Committees are spokesmen for tobacco and rice interests respectively. This not only gives those crops valuable support, but also discourages other interests from opposing them lest they should alienate such important legislators. Conflict is further minimized if the crop interests are small, wealthy businesses. The relative size and wealth of truck farmers, for example, enables them to exert pressure on Congress while attracting a minimum of public attention. The kind of program advocated bears also on the degree of conflict generated. Compare, for example, "marketing order" programs with price support programs. Proponents of a marketing order need not request Congress to review the details of a plan and vote subsidies to support it, but only to authorize the Secretary of Agriculture to enforce the marketing restriction plans designed and approved by the growers. And once established, marketing order programs are rarely reconsidered in Congress since they do not require periodic appropriations. Thus, the growers of many, smaller, more specialized crops—because of procedures which attract little attention thereby minimizing political controversy, and because of the limited amount of government activity involved—have been able to secure beneficial legislation with relative ease.

BROADER INTERESTS?

The conflicts discussed so far have been based on individual crop interests or on interests within a crop. But do larger groups, each of which includes several crop interests, play significant roles in agricultural policy-making? The importance of two kinds of larger groups—the political party and the national farm organization—should be considered.

Political Parties • Since farm policy is one of the few major issues in American politics on which the Republican and Democratic Party platforms clearly differ, and since roll call votes in Congress look partisan, party membership appears to be an important determinant of politicians' behavior on farm price support bills. If, however, the makeup of the parties is examined, this behavior can be as easily explained on the theory that crop interests are the dominant forces. The congressional delegations representing each crop tend to be found in one party or the other. A survey of the party affiliation of Congressmen representing districts ranking in the top twenty in the production of each of several crops indicates the following pattern:

Crop	Democrats	Republicans
Rice	20	0
Peanuts	20	0
Cotton	20	1
Tobacco	17	3
Wheat	7	14
Dairy	4	16
Corn	2	18

Most rice, peanut, cotton, and tobacco producers have in common the desire for programs of production restrictions and price supports. The Democratic Party, with which they are affiliated, espouses these programs. Similarly, many dairymen and corn-hog farmers favor fewer controls, and embrace the Republican Party, which advocates this approach. Moreover, although there are conflicts among the crops within each party, the differences in crop interests between the two parties are greater. For example, some Southern (Democratic) crop interests conflict with Midwestern (Republican) interests because their products compete. Party regularity on congressional votes is, therefore, often consistent with the following of constituency interests.

Indeed, the nature of the particular crop interests within each party probably determines the party's agricultural policy. The case of wheat is instructive. Although one would expect wheat farmers to be aligned with the Democrats because wheat has a chronic problem of oversupply, of the top twenty wheat districts, fourteen have Republican Congressmen. However, these Republicans are a substantial portion of those few party members who occasionally stray from the official party position and vote for the Democrats' programs. Furthermore, the Democrats have been making substantial gains in wheat districts in recent years. In wheat therefore, the crop, not the party interest seems dominant. The two available studies on the problem support a generalized statement of this conclusion. A study of several roll calls on price-support bills during the period 1949–1955 found that Congressmen followed constituency interests to a greater degree than party. And a more recent study concludes that the pull of party as compared with constituency influences is even less strong in congressional committee maneuvering than it is in final roll call votes on the floor. In the agriculture committees, where most of the important compromises between crop interests must be worked out if a bill is to succeed, the unifying effect of party discipline is weaker, and loyalty to narrow crop interests is greater. There the impasse in agricultural policymaking has its roots.

National Farm Organizations • National farm organizations represent broad segments of the farm population, and therefore each includes many crop interests. The oldest and largest of these organizations are the American Farm Bureau Federation (AFBF), the National Farmers Union (NFU), and the National Grange. More recently the National Conference of Commodity Organizations and the National Farm Organization have been formed. The two organizations most influential politically, the AFBF and the NFU, have consistently been at odds on agricultural policy. But, as with the two parties, this conflict may be explained in terms of crop interests. Most crops affiliated with the AFBF— livestock, corn-livestock, and big cotton—would be benefitted by Republican free market policies, while the dominant crop interest in the NFU—wheat—depends on price support programs advocated by the Democrats. The conflicts among crops within each organization are less pronounced than the crop-based conflicts between the two organizations. Paradoxically, consistency in the policy positions expressed by the leaders of each organization may be a result of the multiplicity of internal conflicts. Since none of the many factions are strong enough to challenge the national leadership, entrenched organization spokesmen are usually able to disregard with impunity the objections of individual crops. While the dissidents are free to resign their membership, they rarely do so because of fringe benefits such as cheap insurance, cooperative buying and marketing, and social and educational programs.

As in those even larger conglomerations of interests, the major political parties, there is much evidence that the pronunciamentos of the national offices of the major farm organizations carry as much weight as the particular crop interests that they benefit, and no more. State Bureaus of the AFBF often appear at Congressional hearings to oppose the position of the national organization when it conflicts with the interests of crops in their own states. But, even stronger evidence of the importance of particular crop interests as opposed to the organizational entity can be found in the experience of the National Conference of Commodity Organizations (NCCO). The NCCO, a confederation of existing single-crop organizations such as the National Milk Producers Federation and the Association of Virginia Peanut and Hog Growers, was formed in 1957 in reaction to the impasse on farm legislation. The idea was that through a series of compromises by the member crop organizations, a single bill, agreed to by all, could be presented to Congress in 1958. Many of the interests of member crops, however, conflicted with each other. Since each member got less than it wanted, all had a general reluctance to press the final bill on the Congressmen with whom they had special influence. The bill failed, as did the NCCO a year later, demonstrating not only the dominance of narrow crop interests, but also the intensity of conflict among them. . . .

This proliferation of interests within agriculture has created a stalemate on farm policy. Congressional procedures are such that a concerted minority interest can usually block action distasteful to it through various obstructive tactics, if the interest has sufficient access to strategic points in the legislative process. Many farm interests have access through the agriculture committees, without whose approval no farm bill is likely to be adopted. The proliferation of interests has meant that there are now many groups, each trying to obstruct the other's programs. The sum of all these obstructionist tactics has been impasse.

PART THREE

Techniques of Regulation

Antitrust is Pro-Business

LEE LOEVINGER

When he wrote this article Lee Loevinger was Assistant Attorney General in charge of the Antitrust Division of the Justice Department. He is now a member of the Federal Communications Commission.

Is THE PRESENT administration of the antitrust laws a fire-breathing dragon threatening business, especially big business, and thus antagonistic to free enterprise, or is it merely a paper tiger intent on watching mouseholes for minor violators while oblivious to the lumbering tread of elephantine monopolies? The first view has been reflected recently in the business press, where terms such as "anti-business," "wild," and "fanatic" have been used to describe the current trustbusters. On the other hand, a liberal Senator recently expressed the second view, characterizing current antitrust enforcement as "toothless" and suggesting it was ineffective and inactive in attacking big business monopolies.

The facts support neither view. The antitrust laws themselves are the foundation and the bulwark of the free-enterprise system. Those in charge of enforcing the antitrust laws understand this thoroughly and apply the laws to achieve this purpose. The present administration of antitrust is both thoroughly pro-business and steadfastly anti-monopoly. . . .

THE OBJECTIVES OF ANTITRUST

In a broad view the antitrust laws are statutory statements of ideals of the American people. Although there is infinite variety of detail possible, there are few fundamentally different methods by which society can achieve its economic aims. All involve the existence of laws that control or limit economic activity in some degree. Any society that has a business and economic system is based upon legal order. Most business enterprises, such as corporations, partnerships, trusts, and joint ventures, are creations of law, as are such elements of business as money and credit, bills and notes, contracts, property, and, most basic of all, the reasonable expectation of law and order. The law, which creates these economic instruments, also specifies their use and limitations.

Basically, there are three legal methods of doing this. The first is by a limitation on the form and extent of economic power. This is the method of competition or free enterprise. The second is by government's determination of the standards of economic performance, made effective either by the imposition of sanctions for failure to comply or by the offer of incentives for compliance. This is the method of regulation. The third alternative is the control of economic institutions by government through ownership. This is the method of socialism.

All governments utilize some elements of each method to some extent. In the United States the Post Office is owned by the government and may be regarded as a socialized enterprise. The transportation industry is largely subject to government control, and is an example of the method of regulation. However, with respect to the greater part of the economy, the American method is that of free competitive enterprise maintained by the antitrust laws.

The first and most obvious objective of the antitrust laws is to avoid exploitation of the consumer by maintaining reasonable prices and good quality. It is assumed this can best be achieved by the maintenance of competition.

The second objective is economic efficiency, which is thought to result from an impersonal and automatic control of prices, products, quality of goods, and, perhaps most important, the allocation of manpower and resources. Our economic system is based on the premise that the automatic and impersonal action of the free market is likely to be more effective and more efficient in the long run than personal judgment, whether exercised through governmental power or through private monopoly.

The third objective is to ensure technological and economic progress by full utilization of the diversity that a free competitive market offers. Our great resource of individual inventiveness and personal initiative can be fully utilized only in a free-enterprise system. Under a system of cartels or monopolies, inventions and technological innovations ordinarily will be employed only by the cartel or monopoly with established power over the relevant field. As one of our greatest judges, Learned Hand, has said, the Sherman Act is based on these premises: ". . . that possession of unchallenged economic power deadens initiative, discourages thrift and depresses energy; that immunity from competition is a narcotic, and rivalry is a stimulant, to industrial progress . . ."

Fourth, by preventing concentration and thus maintaining dispersal of economic power, the antitrust laws lay the foundation and secure the conditions for preserving political democracy and civil liberties. In an economy composed of a single monopoly or a series of cartels, an individual skilled in a business, craft, or profession might find only a single employer. The overwhelming majority of citizens would then find their personal freedom wholly dependent on the tolerance of their employer. Precisely this situation exists in countries with a wholly socialized economy. Private monopoly is merely slightly less extensive in its effect. In the words of a recent opinion of the United States Supreme Court, "The Sherman Act was designed to be a comprehensive charter of economic liberty."

Finally, by seeking to maintain and preserve economic freedom the antitrust laws secure something valued as an end in itself. The American people believe freedom to be inherently good and to be an essential part of that ethical system in which the ultimate standard of value is the welfare of the individual.

What the laws prohibit • As modern industrial society is complex, so are the laws that govern it. The antitrust laws are numerous and involve many special rules for specific situations and some immunities and partial exemptions. Basically, however, four simple principles are involved.

The first and most general principle, in Section 1 of the Sherman Act, is that all contracts, combinations, and conspiracies in restraint of trade are prohibited. Here the word "trade" means competition. The second, in Section 2 of the Sherman Act, is that it is unlawful to monopolize, attempt to monopolize, or combine to monopolize. The third, in Section 7 of the Clayton Act, is that no corporation shall acquire or merge with any other corporation where the effect may be to lessen competition substantially or tend to create a monopoly.

The fourth principle is in the Robinson-Patman Act, which is an amendment to Section 2 of the Clayton Act. This prohibits discrimination in price between purchasers of the same commodity where the effect may be to lessen competition or tend toward monopoly. The act permits price differentials that make due allowance for differing costs arising from different conditions of sale, and it also specifies a number of detailed rules as to what is discriminatory.

There are some additional substantive provisions in the antitrust laws, such as the prohibitions against tying agreements and against interlocking directorates. But these are merely efforts to specify particular practices that Congress regards as restrictive of competition.

How cases are selected • The basic antitrust enforcement policy of this Administration is to achieve the objectives of the law by compliance. It does not seek to impose penalties upon business, to secure injunctions, or to win cases just for the sake of a statistical record. Were the program of enforcement perfectly effective, there would be universal voluntary compliance and litigation would be confined entirely to borderline cases in which the application of general principles required judicial determination. No such utopian condition seems imminent or prospective. However, such a hypothesis emphasizes the point that statistical measures of cases filed are not a good indication of the effectiveness of enforcement activity.

With respect to the specific cases that are brought, there is an inescapable burden of selection imposed by the limitations of manpower and money. There always are more complaints than it is possible to investigate fully and more potential cases than it is possible to prosecute.

Within this area of discretion, cases are now selected on the basis of economic significance and potential contribution to the achievement of antitrust objectives. Enforcement activity is not fashioned to fit any preconceived ideas as to which sections of law should be enforced or which areas of business should be prosecuted. While errors of judgment are always possible, enforcement policy now is guided solely by the policy and standards of the statutes on the basis of the specific facts in each case. Despite some published opinions to the contrary, enforcement policy and activity during the past year have been neither hostile to business nor punitive. For example, the proportion of criminal cases to total cases filed in 1961 was the lowest of any year in the last decade. (See table.)

The Antitrust Scorecard

Year	Total cases filed	Civil	Criminal	Price fixing	Mergers (Section 7 Clayton Act)	Individuals indicted
1961	60	41	19	28	18*	44
1960	90	57	33	70	11	53
1959	63	29	34	42	10	54
1958	59	33	26	33	5	25
1957	56	30	26	34	1	57
1956	46	29	17	25	6	55
1955	54	33	21	25	5	81
1954	34	23	11	12	—	37
1953	29	10	19	21	—	73
1952	36	24	12	13	—	58
1951	49	35	14	29	—	62

* Another anti-merger case was brought under the Sherman Act.

Law enforcement does not, and should not, involve the promulgation of policy at all. It is rather the expression of the official view of the law. So some of the questions concerning enforcement can be answered best by discussing specific aspects of the law.

ARE ANTITRUST STANDARDS UNCERTAIN?

Businessmen and their spokesmen sometimes claim the antitrust laws are too indefinite and uncertain. They say that this uncertainty makes it difficult or impossible to comply with antitrust standards. On the other hand, some business critics, often the same ones who claim uncertainty, also assert that the laws are too rigid and inflexible. It should be evident that it is impossible for laws to be both flexible and uncertain at the same time.

The antitrust laws combine both flexibility and certainty, both generality and detail, as do must of our important laws. The basic principles are stated in broad general terms, requiring interpretations by application to specific situations. Thus decisions in specific cases build a body of judicial precedents that supplements the statutes and provides guides to the meaning of the laws.

This is the common-law method of developing legal doctrine and is fundamental to our system of government. For example, the legal principle of most common and general application is the rule imposing liability for negligence. This rule states generally that anyone who fails to exercise the care of a reasonable man and thereby injures another must pay for the damages caused. This is a principle of wide application stated in simple and general terms and most flexible in its application. The interpretation or application of this principle has given rise to literally tens of thousands of cases that give specific content to the general rule.

Similarly, the Sherman Act is a charter of freedom that, in the words of Chief Justice Charles Evans Hughes, "has a generality and adaptability comparable to that found to be desirable in constitutional provisions. It does not go into detailed definitions which might either work injury to legitimate enterprise or through particularization defeat its purposes by providing loopholes for escape. The restrictions the act imposes are not mechanical or artificial."

Early in the history of the antitrust laws, the Supreme Court declared that the Sherman Act was to be applied in a reasonable manner, which would not interfere with the conduct of business by all normal methods, but would prohibit all acts and practices that restrained competition. Over the years the courts have recognized that certain practices are of a kind the statute was clearly intended to prohibit. Thus the Supreme Court has held that certain acts are unreasonable per se and therefore illegal. These are principally price fixing of every kind, agreements among competitors for the allocation of customers or territories, group boycotts, the pooling of profits by competitors, and other similar types of agreements not to compete.

Regarding these practices, there is great certainty and little flexibility. On the other hand, practices that are not per se unreasonable must be judged by their purposes and probable effects in the light of all relevant economic circumstances. For these, there is considerable flexibility but correspondingly less certainty.

WHAT IS A MONOPOLY?

Enforcement of the Sherman Act provisions prohibiting monopoly inevitably involves some flexibility. Monopoly is a situation in which a single seller has complete control of the supply of a commodity in a given market. In real economic existence, such a situation is seldom, if ever, found. To pose a paradox, in theory monopoly is a practical concept, but in practice it is a theoretical one. In practice a single seller controlling the entire supply of a commodity is rarely found because the concepts of both commodity and market are so broad that there is nearly always some degree of competition with even an apparently monopolized product. Thus in the famous cellophane case the Supreme Court held that du Pont did not have an illegal monopoly of cellophane, although it was the dominant manufacturer, because the "relevant market" included many other flexible packaging materials that were competitive with cellophane.

The courts do not deal in terms of perfect competition or complete monopoly, but practical applications of these concepts. As long ago as 1911, in the Standard Oil case, the Supreme Court said that the Sherman Act forbids "all contracts or acts which [are] unreasonably restrictive of competitive conditions." In the same case the Court referred to "substantial power over the . . . product" as amounting to monopoly. In a series of subsequent decisions the Court has made plain that monopoly is the power to control the price of a product or to exclude competition from a market.

There is no quantitative test to identify monopoly, and indeed the concept of economic power itself cannot be analyzed directly by objective criteria. Unfortunately, no objective or operational criterion of monopoly has been furnished by economics or any of the social sciences. While legal standards are vague, their applications in prior decided cases gives them at least as much precision as the definitions provided by other disciplines for such concepts as competition and monopoly.

The Department of Justice continues to be guided by the Supreme Court's statement in the 1932 Swift case that: "Mere size . . . is not an offense against the Sherman Act unless magnified to the point at which it amounts to a monopoly . . . but size carries with it an opportunity for abuse that is not to be ignored when the opportunity is proved to have been utilized in the past."

Market power is recognized as an economic circumstance that is relevant in some, but not in other, antitrust cases. Practices such as price fixing, which are unreasonable per se, are equally forbidden for all business, whether big or small in market power. On the other hand, a far wider range of practices is prohibited only where they appear to be unreasonable in the setting of economic circumstances. In such cases the relative market size of the enterprise involved clearly is important. An acquisition or merger by a company already very large in relation to its market is far more likely to lessen competition substantially or tend to create a monopoly in violation of the antitrust laws than a similar transaction by a small company. But size alone is not controlling. For example, in a recent case the Antitrust Division acquiesced in the merger of two large oil companies, Standard Oil of California and Standard Oil Co. (Kentucky). The situation was such that the merger would create new competition in an area previously dominated by a larger oil company, Standard Oil of New Jersey. The introduction of new competition outweighed the increased market power of Socal and Kyso and consequently was thought to be consistent with antitrust objectives. Competition, rather than size, is the ultimate criterion.

Although we cannot formulate any exact quantitative definition of monopoly, we can thus establish standards in terms of intent, of conduct, and of the maintenance of competitive market conditions that serve as reasonable guideposts from case to case and mark out the area of illegal monopoly power.

THE ANTITRUST GUIDEPOSTS

The Department of Justice seeks to give as much assistance as it properly can to businessmen who are attempting to comply with the antitrust laws. The department is not authorized to give advisory opinions to private persons or enterprises. However, it has a program, which has been in existence for a number of years, that permits the submission of matters to the Antitrust Division for "release" or "clearance" letters.

Antitrust "release" letters permit an advance review of business plans or proposed programs to ascertain whether they involve risk of criminal prosecution if adopted. The procedure is relatively simple and informal. Its elements are these:

1. A request for a release or clearance letter must be submitted in writing to the Department of Justice.

2. The submission must contain a full disclosure regarding a specific business proposal. If additional facts or data concerning the proposal are sought by the Antitrust Division, the information must be supplied upon request.

3. The submission must relate to a plan or program that is purely prospective and not operative. No consideration will be given to a request for an expression as to operations that are being conducted at the time.

4. The facts and plans disclosed must affirmatively show that the plan and the proposed operations will be fully consistent with the antitrust laws.

5. In the event of such a submission and showing, a release letter will be issued waiving the government's right to institute criminal proceedings against the parties involved.

6. In the event of a submission that does not affirmatively show that the plan and proposed operations will be fully consistent with the antitrust laws, the government may refuse to take a position or make any comment upon the proposal; or it may advise the parties that the proposal appears to be contrary to the antitrust laws, if that is the case.

7. The government in any event reserves the right to institute civil proceedings if it appears that the legality of the activities or program in question should be tested.

8. If the plan in actual operation or the activities engaged in go beyond the statements set forth in the submission, or if there was not a full disclosure in the submission made to the Department of Justice, the government reserves the right to proceed either civilly or criminally.

9. The submission of a request for a release or clearance letter does not prejudice the position or any right of the party making the submission. The submission may be withdrawn prior to the issuance of a letter. An unfavorable opinion by the Department of Justice is not binding, and does not legally preclude the proposed action if the party making the submission is prepared to defend the action in court.

10. The submission of a request for a release or clearance letter

does not by itself create any immunity from prosecution, and such submission does not preclude the government from taking any action that may be appropriate upon the basis of facts disclosed. Release and clearance commitments are given only in formal written communications. Such commitments are never given and are not authorized to be made except in writing over the signature of a responsible official of the Department of Justice.

Although the government's commitment under the release program is limited to a waiver of its right to proceed in a criminal case, as a practical matter such a letter will seldom, if ever, be issued if the staff of the Antitrust Division believes that either a civil or a criminal proceeding should be instituted on the basis of the proposal submitted.

MINIMIZING UNCERTAINTY

The merger-clearance program differs chiefly in the nature of the commitment, since legal actions against mergers are, except in the most extraordinary cases, civil rather than criminal. Under the merger-clearance program the submission and disclosure required are the same as under the release program mentioned above. Where the Antitrust Division finds that a proposed merger does not raise serious questions under the antitrust laws, it may issue a "clearance letter" stating the antitrust laws, it may issue a "clearance letter" stating that the department does not intend to take legal action against the merger if consummated, but that it reserves the right to institute action later if subsequent developments or operations involve antitrust violations.

The Department of Justice cannot answer abstract or hypothetical questions, but it does seek by the release and clearance program to give businessmen as much assurance as possible under the antitrust laws and to minimize the inevitable area of uncertainty that is involved in the application of all law. . . .

COMPETITION IS GOOD FOR BUSINESS

Some businessmen, in both America and Europe, would prefer to avoid competition. This is understandable. Competition requires effort and ability; it poses a constant threat of failure for indifference, indolence, or incompetence. Cartels and monopolies promise assured profits without requiring commensurate effort, ability, or achievement. Nevertheless, competition, and the qualities that sustain it, have been the foundation of American business and American achievement. As President Kennedy said, ". . . trade and competition and innovation have long been a significant part of the American character." There is increasing recognition today in Great Britain and in continental Europe, as in the United States, that cartels and monopoly breed economic stagnation and weakness, while competition leads to economic vigor, progress, and prosperity.

Thus the antitrust laws and their enforcement, by protecting and strengthening the role of competition, are truly and profoundly pro-business. This is demonstrated by the fact that of more than 1,200 complaints received by the Antitrust Division each year over two-thirds are from businessmen—small, middle-sized, and big businessmen. The great majority of antitrust investigations and of cases filed under the antitrust laws are the result of requests by business for this legal protection.

All businessmen should realize, as many do, that by keeping the economy free, by preventing restrictive and unfair practices, by protecting competition, and by permitting equality of opportunity for all, antitrust enforcement maintains the conditions that permit and foster the growth of American business.

The Crisis in Antitrust

ROBERT H. BORK AND WARD S. BOWMAN, JR.

Robert H. Bork and Ward S. Bowman, Jr. are both members of the Faculty of the Yale Law School.

Long-standing contradictions at the root of antitrust doctrine have today brought it to a crisis of policy. From its inception with the passage of the Sherman Act in 1890, antitrust has vacillated between the policy of preserving competition and the policy of preserving competitors from their more energetic and efficient rivals. It is the rapid acceleration of the latter "protectionist" trends in antitrust that has brought on the present crisis. Anti-free-market forces now have the upper hand and are steadily broadening and consolidating their victory. The continued acceptance and expansion of their doctrine, which now constitutes antitrust's growing edge, threaten within the foreseeable future to destroy the antitrust laws as guarantors of a competitive economy.

The situation would be sufficiently serious if antitrust were merely a set of economic prescriptions applicable to a sector of the economy, but it is much more than that; it is also an expression of a social philosophy, an educative force, and a political symbol of extraordinary potency. Its capture by the opponents of the free market is thus likely to have effects far beyond the confines of antitrust itself.

The very existence of this crisis—and the basic societal changes it portends—seems unsuspected by most Americans. Even the general business community, which will be most directly affected, though it is conscious of hostility, appears to understand neither the nature nor the immediacy of the threat. To be sure, businessmen and their lawyers may frequently be heard inveighing against some particular action of the courts or of the governmental enforcement agencies. Calls from industry for mutual reasonableness and understanding between government and business are common. But such responses to the situation are dangerously beside the point. The problem is not created by a temporary aberration of the courts or the unreasonableness of a particular set of officials who can be jollied out of it or, if not, who will eventually be replaced with a more reasonable crew. The danger arises from a fundamental and widespread misconception of the nature and virtues of the competitive process. This misconception, coupled occasionally with real hostility toward the free market, exists in varying degrees in the courts, in the governmental enforcement agencies, and in the Congress, with the result that in crucial areas the doctrines of antitrust are performing a 180-degree turn away from competition.

The nature of the present crisis in the law can be demonstrated by comparing the law concerning price fixing and the developing law of mergers. The comparison illustrates the schizophrenia afflicting basic antitrust policy.

The rule that price fixing and similar cartel arrangements are illegal *per se*, that is, incapable of legal justification, must be ranked one of the greatest accomplishments of antitrust. Though its wisdom may seem obvious now, it was not always apparent that this was the correct rule or that the courts would adopt it. The first price-fixing case to reach the Supreme Court (in 1897) was the government's Sherman Act suit against the Trans-Missouri Freight Association, an association of railroads that agreed upon rates to be charged shippers. Both the trial court and the court of appeals agreed that the government's bill should be dismissed because the agreement provided for "reasonable" rates and the new Sherman Act only struck down unreasonable restraints of trade. The Supreme Court, by a five-to-four vote, rejected this view. If one vote had been cast the other way the "reasonableness" of the price agreed upon would have determined legality and the Sherman Act might easily have become not the symbol of the free market but a judicial version of the NRA. To many observers at the time the Supreme Court's Trans-Missouri decision seemed disastrous. Were businessmen to be helpless to defend themselves by reasonable agreement from "ruinous competition"? Would not the small and perhaps less efficient producer be at the mercy of the more efficient? The Supreme Court majority rejected such arguments for judicially supervised cartels. A year later William Howard Taft, then a circut-court judge, rejected a similar defense in the Addyston Pipe & Steel case, saying that to adopt such a standard was to "set sail on a sea of

doubt" and that courts that had done it had "assumed the power
to say . . . how much restraint of competition is in the public
interest, and how much is not." Since then, with very few exceptions, the Supreme Court has hewed to the rule of *per se* illegality
for cartel agreements.

The reason behind the characterization of this rule as one of
the supreme achievements of antitrust goes straight to fundamen-
tals. Why should we want to preserve competition anyway? The
answer is simply that it is the chief glory of competition that it
gives society the maximum output that can be achieved at any
given time with the resources at its command. Under a competitive regime productive resources are combined and separated,
shuffled and reshuffled ever anew in the endless search for
greater profits through greater efficiency. Each productive resource moves to that employment where the value of its marginal
product, and hence the return paid to it, is greatest. Output is
seen to be maximized because there is no possible rearrangement
of resources that could increase the value to consumers of total
output. We want competition, then, because we want our society
to be as rich as possible and because we want individual consumers to determine by their actions what goods and services
they want most. This preference for material prosperity requires
no apology. Aside from its obvious advantages, prosperity is important both in our long-run competition with the Communist
world and for humanitarian reasons. There is much justifiable
concern about relative poverty in our society and about particular
groups that are thought to be disadvantaged in one way or another. It should be obvious that such groups will achieve major
gains in prosperity only by sharing in the general increase of
wealth. Competition allows us to use our resources most effectively to this end.

Price fixing is antisocial precisely because it lessens the total
output of the society. When competitors agree on higher prices
and put them into effect, they necessarily restrict output and so
reduce total wealth. Some of the resources in the industry are
then unused or are forced to migrate to other employment where
the value placed on them by consumers is not so high. Over time,
of course, such resources will move back into the industry as new
firms, attracted by the higher rate of return there, move in. Usually the only way for the cartelists to prevent that is to persuade

the government to impose legal barriers on entry into the industry, but that is not always possible. The tendency of competition to erode cartels does not, however, disprove the value of the rule against price fixing. Though its life is limited, the cartel may last long enough to cause a substantial loss in output.

The *per se* rule fashioned by the Supreme Court is thus a model antitrust law. It is at once a clear, workable rule and the expression of sound social policy. In dismal contrast has been the record of the courts in the field of mergers and of practices that are thought to injure competition by injuring competitors. Such practices as exclusive dealing and price discrimination fall within this latter category. It is here that antitrust has gone awry and that the immediate cause of its crisis lies. In order to understand the crisis, it is essential to understand the doctrines that underlie the courts' performance. These consist primarily of the theories of: (1) monopoly-gaining or exclusionary practices; (2) incipiency; and (3) the "social" purposes of the antitrust law. Though they enjoy nearly universal acceptance and provide the impetus and intellectual support for the law's current growth, these doctrines in their present form are demonstrably fallacious in concept and visibly hurtful in application.

Economic theory indicates that present notions of the exclusionary practices are fallacious. This was first perceived by Professor Aaron Director, of the University of Chicago Law School, who noted that practices conventionally labeled "exclusionary" —notably, price discrimination, vertical mergers, exclusive-dealing contracts, and the like—appeared to be either competitive tactics equally available to all firms or means of maximizing the returns from a market position already held. Director's analysis indicates that, absent special factors which have not been shown to exist, so-called exclusionary practices are not means of injuring the competitive process. The example of requirements contracts (i.e., contracts by which a customer agrees to take all his requirements of a product from a particular supplier) can be used to illustrate the point. The theory of exclusionary tactics underlying the law appears to be that firm X, which already has 10 percent of the market, can sign up more than 10 percent of the retailers, perhaps 20 percent, and, by thus "foreclosing" rivals from retail outlets, obtain a larger share of the market. One must then ask why so many retailers are willing to limit themselves to selling

X's product. Why do not 90 percent of them turn to X's rivals? Because X has greater market acceptance? But then X's share of the market would grow for that reason and the requirements contracts have nothing to do with it. Because X offers them some extra inducement? But that sounds like competition, it is equivalent to a price cut, and surely X's competitors can be relied upon to meet competition.

The theory of exclusionary practices, here exemplified in the use of requirements contracts, seems to require one of two additional assumptions to be made theoretically plausible. One is the assumption that there are practices by which a competitor can impose greater costs upon his rivals than upon himself. That would mean that X could somehow make it more expensive for his rivals to sign retailers to requirements contracts than it is for X to do so. It would be as though X could offer a retailer a $1 price reduction and it would cost any rival $2 to match the offer. It is difficult to imagine that such a mechanism exists in the case of requirements, price cutting, or the usual examples of predatory or exclusionary practices, but it is perhaps conceivable. One possibility, though of limited applicability, would be the case where the only seller of a full line required retailers to deal with him exclusively or not at all. He might be able to get more retailers than his initial market share would seem to command if it would be difficult or impossible for the retailers to assemble a full line from the remaining suppliers.

The other assumption upon which the theory of exclusionary practices might rest is that there are imperfections in or difficulties of access to the capital market that enable X to offer a $1 inducement (it has a bankroll) and prevent its rivals from responding (they have no bankroll and, though the offering of the inducement is a responsible business tactic, for some reason cannot borrow the money). No general case has been made showing that imperfections of this type exist in the capital market.

MYTH AND FACT IN THE STANDARD OIL CASE

Professor Director's reasoning applies to all practices thought to be exclusionary or monopoly gaining. A moment's thought indicates, moreover, that the notion of exclusionary practices is not merely theoretically weak but is, for such a widely accepted idea, remarkably lacking in factual support. Has anybody ever seen a firm gain a monopoly or anything like one through the use of requirements contracts? Or through price discrimination? One may begin to suspect that antitrust is less a science than an elaborate mythology, that it has operated for years on hearsay and legends rather than on reality. The few supposedly verified cases of the successful use of exclusionary tactics to achieve monopoly are primarily in the early history of antitrust. The story of the old Standard Oil trust is probably the classic example. The Supreme Court's 1911 Standard Oil opinion is pivotal not merely because it is thought to have launched the famous "rule of reason," nor because it decreed dissolution which made the oil industry more competitive. Its greatest significance is that it gave weight, substance, and seeming historical veracity to the whole theory of exclusionary and monopoly-gaining techniques. It thus provided much of the impetus for the passage of the Clayton and Federal Trade Commission acts in 1914. Such intellectual support as can be mustered for the law against price discrimination derives primarily from the lessons supposedly taught by that case.

The factual accuracy of the Standard Oil legend is under attack and is coming to seem as dubious as the theory that it is thought to support. Professor John McGee, an economist now at Duke University, reviewed the entire case record of the Standard Oil litigation and reported that there is not one clear episode of the successful use by Standard Oil of local price cutting or other predatory practices. The other supposed instances of monopolies gained through such tactics deserve similar investigation.

It would be claiming too much to say that there is no merit to the theory of exclusionary practices, but it is fair to say that that theory has been seriously challenged at both the theoretical and the empirical levels. Perhaps a sound theoretical base can be constructed. The law could then be directed at those practices that in particular settings may be exclusionary. So far as is known, however, this task has not been undertaken or even recognized by the Antitrust Division, the Federal Trade Commission, or any court.

The incipiency theory starts from the idea that it is possible to nip restraints of trade and monopolies in the bud before they blossom to Sherman Act proportions. It underlies the Clayton

Act, the Robinson-Patman Act, and the Federal Trade Commission Act. Though the idea initially sounds plausible, its consequences have proved calamitous. The courts have used the incipiency notion as a license for almost unlimited extrapolation, reasoning from any trend toward concentration in an industry that there is an incipient lessening of competition. The difficulty with stopping a trend toward a more concentrated condition at a very early stage is that the existence of the trend is prima facie evidence that greater concentration is socially desirable. The trend indicates that there are emerging efficiencies or economies of scale—whether due to engineering and production developments or to new control and management techniques—which make larger size more efficient. This increased efficiency is valuable to the society at large, for it means that fewer of our available resources are being used to accomplish the same amount of production and distribution. By striking at such trends in their very earliest stages the concept of incipiency prevents the realization of those very efficiencies that competition is supposed to encourage. But it is when the incipiency concept works in tandem with the unsophisticated theory of exclusionary practices currently in use that its results are most anticompetitive. Where a court or the Federal Trade Commission lacks the means to distinguish between tactics that impose greater costs on rivals and those that are normal means of competing, what evidence can it look to in its effort to discern an incipient lessening of competition? The obvious resort is to evidence that a competitor has been injured, for it is through the infliction of injury upon competitors that the exclusionary devices are thought ultimately to injure the competitive process itself. There seems no way to tell that a competitor has been "injured," however, except that he has lost business. And this is precisely the meaning that the statutory test of incipient lessening of competition or tendency toward monopoly is coming to have. In case after case the FTC, for example, nails down its finding that competition is injured with the testimony of competitors of the respondent that his activities and aggressiveness may or have cost them sales. The conduct that threatens such "injury" is then prohibited. That this result is itself profoundly anticompetitive seems never to occur to the commission or to most courts.

When the anti-efficiency impact of the law is occasionally

perceived, the third theory—the social purpose of the antitrust laws—is called upon to provide a rationalization. Judge Learned Hand's Alcoa opinion contains the most famous exposition of this view. Hand suggested that Congress, in passing the Sherman Act, had not necessarily been actuated by economic motives alone, and continued: "It is possible, because of its indirect social or moral effect, to prefer a system of small producers, each dependent for his success upon his own skill and character, to one in which the great mass of those engaged must accept the direction of a few." He went on to say: "Throughout the history of these statutes it has been constantly assumed that one of their purposes was to perpetuate and preserve, for its own sake and in spite of possible cost, an organization of industry in small units which can effectively compete with each other."

Hand's rhetoric has commended itself to most commentators on the topic, but it seems clear upon reflection that it is a position which is inaccurate as a description of congressional intent, dubious as social policy, and impossible as antitrust doctrine.

It is simply not accurate to say that Congress ever squarely decided to prefer the preservation of small business to the preservation of a free market in which the forces of competition worked themselves out. There was much rhetoric in Congress about the virtues of small business but no clear indication that antitrust should create shelters for the inefficient. In fact, the statutory language of all the major antitrust laws after the Sherman Act explicitly requires the preservation of *competition*. That places an enormous burden of persuasion upon those who purport to find in the legislative history a direction to value small business above competition.

Hand's notion, moreover, is dubious, and indeed radical, social policy. It would be hard to demonstrate that the independent druggist or groceryman is any more solid and virtuous a citizen than the local manager of a chain operation. The notion that such persons are entitled to special consideration has typified some of the ugliest European social movements. It hardly seems suited to the United States, whose dominant ideal, though doubtless often enough flouted in practice, has been that each business should survive only by serving consumers as they want to be served. If that ideal is to be departed from here, if antitrust is to turn from its role as the maintainer of free markets to become the industrial and commercial equivalent of the farm price-support program, then we are entitled to an unequivocal policy choice by Congress and not to vague philosophizing by judges who lack the qualifications and the mandate to behave as philosopher kings.

It is clear, in addition, that the "social purpose" concept is impossible as antitrust doctrine. It runs into head-on conflict with the *per se* rules against cartel agreements. Those rules leave it entirely to the play of competitive forces to determine which competitors shall grow and which shall shrink and disappear. If the social-policy argument makes sense, then we had better drop the *per se* rule in favor of one permitting the defense that cartels benefit small businessmen. Co-existence of the social-policy argument with the pro-competitive rules would introduce so vague a factor that prediction of the courts' behavior would become little more than a guessing game. How could one know in a particular case whether the court would apply a rigorously pro-competitive rule or the social policy of preserving small business units from aggressive behavior? When the person whose conduct is to be judged is in doubt concerning which of two completely contradictory policies will be applied, the system hardly deserves the name of law.

THE CRASH OF MERGER POLICY

The three theories discussed are active in many areas of antitrust, but perhaps they may be best illustrated in the law that is now developing under the antimerger statute, amended Section 7 of the Clayton Act. Their collaboration produced the crash of antitrust merger policy in Chief Justice Warren's opinion for the Supreme Court in Brown Shoe Company *v.* United States. The Court there held illegal the merger of Brown, primarily a shoe manufacturer, with the G. R. Kinney Company, primarily a retailer. Their respective shares of the nation's shoe output were 4 percent and 0.5 percent. Kinney had 1.2 percent of total national retail shoe sales by dollar volume (no figure was given for Brown), and together the companies had 2.3 percent of total retail shoe outlets. With over 800 shoe manufacturers, the industry was as close to pure competition as is possible outside a classroom model. Yet the seven Justices participating in the case managed to see a threat to competition at both the manufacturing and the retailing levels, and they did so by using the three concepts already discussed.

The Court held the merger illegal for both its vertical and its horizontal aspects. The Court generally views vertical integration as a form of exclusionary practice, since it is always possible that the manufacturing level will sell to the retail level of the same firm and thereby "foreclose" a share of the retail market otherwise open to competing manufacturers. In the Brown Shoe case the Court said the share of the market foreclosed was not enough by itself to make the merger illegal but that it became illegal when two other factors were examined: ". . . the trend toward vertical integration in the shoe industry, [and] . . . Brown's avowed policy of forcing its own shoes upon its retail subsidiaries . . ." It is enlightening to examine the facts upon which that conclusion rests. The "trend toward vertical integration" was seen in the fact that a number of manufacturers had acquired retailing chains. The district court found that the thirteen largest shoe manufacturers, for example, operated 21 percent of the census shoe stores. Accepting that figure for the moment, it is impossible to see any harm to competition. On a straight extrapolation, there would be room for over sixty manufacturers of equal size to integrate to the same extent, and that would result in as pure competition as is conceivable. In fact, since these were the largest shoe manufacturers, there would be room for many more manufacturers. But that is by no means all; the category of census shoe stores includes only those that make at least half their income from selling shoes. It thus leaves out about two-thirds of the outlets that actually sell shoes, including such key ones as department and clothing stores. Even if, as there was no reason to expect, complete vertical integration took place in the industry, there would obviously be room for hundreds of shoe manufacturers, and, given the ease of entry into shoe retailing, no basis for imagining that any new manufacturer could not find or create outlets any time he chose. The Court's cited "trend toward vertical integration" was thus impossible to visualize as a threat to competition.

Brown's "avowed policy of forcing its own shoes upon its retail subsidiaries" turns out, upon inspection of the Court's footnotes, to spring from the testimony of its president that Brown's motive in making the deal was to get distribution in a range of prices it was not covering, and also, as Kinney moved into stores in higher income neighborhoods and needed to upgrade and add new lines, ". . . it would give us an opportunity, we hoped, to be able to sell them in that category." The empirical evidence of coercion was no more impressive than this "avowal." At the time of the merger Kinney bought no shoes from Brown, but two years later Brown was supplying 7.9 percent of Kinney's needs. (Brown's sales to its other outlets apparently had risen no higher than 33 percent of requirements, except in one case in which Brown supplied over 50 percent.) The "trend toward vertical integration" and the "avowed policy of forcing its own shoes upon its retail subsidiaries" were thus almost entirely imaginary. But even if they were accepted at face value, it ought to be noted that, since Kinney supplied about 20 percent of its own retail requirements, less than 1 percent of the nation's total retail shoe sales was open to "foreclosure" by Brown through this merger and it had actually "foreclosed" slightly less than one-tenth of 1 percent. The idea of vertical integration as an exclusionary device had to be coupled with almost unlimited extrapolation in the name of incipiency to reach the incredible result that the Court achieved on the vertical aspect of the case.

The horizontal aspect—the putting together of Brown's and Kinney's retail outlets—was held illegal on similar reasoning. The Court found the creation of market shares of as low as 5 percent of shoe retailing in any city illegal, stating: "If a merger achieving 5 percent control were now approved, we might be required to approve future merger efforts by Brown's competitors seeking similar market shares. The oligopoly Congress sought to avoid would then be furthered . . ." On this reasoning every merger "furthers" oligopoly no matter how small a share of the market is taken over. To imagine that every firm would then merge up to 5 percent is to indulge in sheer conjecture, and in any event the result would be competition. Twenty firms in an industry is far too many to act as oligopolists. Given the ease and rapidity of entry into shoe retailing, the Supreme Court's fear of oligopoly is simply incomprehensible.

Then, apparently without realizing the inconsistency with its earlier prediction that Brown would "force" its shoes upon Kinney, the Court suggested that the merger was also bad because Kinney's new ability to get Brown's shoes more cheaply would give it an advantage over other retailers. "The retail outlets of integrated companies, by eliminating wholesalers and by increasing the volume of purchases from the manufacturing division of the enterprise, can market their own brands at prices below those of competing independent retailers." The merger was therefore bad both because Brown might "force" Kinney and because Kinney wanted to be "forced." This fascinating holding creates an antitrust analogue to the crime of statutory rape.

Apparently concerned that the achievement of efficiency and low prices through merger seemed to be illegal under this formulation, the Court then stated: "Of course, some of the results of large integrated or chain operations are beneficial to consumers. Their expansion is not rendered unlawful by the mere fact that small independent stores may be adversely affected. It is competition, not competitors, which the Act protects. But we cannot fail to recognize Congress' desire to promote competition through the protection of viable, small, locally owned businesses. Congress appreciated that occasional higher costs and prices might result from the maintenance of fragmented industries and markets. It resolved these competing considerations in favor of decentralization." No matter how many times you read it, that passage states: Although mergers are not rendered unlawful by the mere fact that small independent stores may be adversely affected, we must recognize that mergers are unlawful when small independent stores may be adversely affected.

The Brown Shoe case employed the theory of exclusionary practices to outlaw vertical integration that promised lower prices, the theory of incipiency to foresee danger in a presumably desirable trend that was barely started, and the theory of "social purpose" to justify the fact that it prevented the realization of efficiencies by a merger that, realistically viewed, did not even remotely threaten competition.

THE ATTACK ON CONGLOMERATES

The FTC and some of the lower federal courts are now pushing these doctrines to their logical conclusion—an attack on efficiency itself as anticompetitive. This is seen most clearly in the rash of suits challenging conglomerate mergers. A conglomerate merger is one between parties that are neither competitors nor related as supplier and customer, an example being the acquisition by a locomotive manufacturer of an underwear maker. It neither increases any firm's share of a market nor forecloses anybody from a market or source of supply. The government's attack on such mergers, therefore, has had to be on the theory that they create a "competitive advantage" which may enable the new firm to injure rivals. The competitive advantage, upon inspection, turns out to be efficiency. Thus a district court recently entered a preliminary injunction at the government's request restraining Ingersoll-Rand Company from acquiring three manufacturers of underground coal-mining machinery and equipment. Though the opinion rested in part upon the competing status of the acquired companies, it stressed the conglomerate aspects of the merger. One of the court's explicit fears was that the merger would create "economies of scale" (efficiencies due to size) which would put other companies at a competitive disadvantage. The court of appeals affirmed, noting as anti-competitive the fact that Ingersoll-Rand would be able "to offer a complete line of equipment to its consumers and to further enhance its position and dominance in the market by extending consumer financing to prospective purchasers through its wholly owned subsidiary finance company." This is a decision that illegality attaches when the merger enables better service to consumers.

On a similar theory the FTC is attacking Proctor & Gamble's acquisition of the Clorox Chemical Company. The hearing examiner has held the acquisition illegal, assigning as major reasons the fact that, by integrating Clorox advertising with its own, P. & G. had realized substantial savings over what Clorox alone had had to spend, and the supposition that P. & G. might sell Clorox through its own existing sales force and thus lower the costs of distribution. The examiner thought the creation of such efficiencies anticompetitive because they might hurt the sales of other liquid-bleach manufacturers. Neither the Ingersoll-Rand case nor the Proctor & Gamble decision considers that the creation of just such efficiencies is the main benefit competition has to offer society. If it now takes fewer salesmen and distribution personnel to move a product from the factory to the consumer than it used to, that is a net gain to society. We are all richer to that extent. Multiply that by hundreds and thousands of transactions and an enormously important social phenomenon is perceived. Any law that makes the creation of efficiency the touch-stone of illegality can only tend to impoverish us as a nation.

PRESERVING THE DODOES

Too few people understand that it is the essential mechanism of competition and its prime virtue that more efficient firms take business away from the less efficient. Some businesses will shrink and some will disappear. Competition is an evolutionary process. Evolution requires the extinction of some species as well as the survival of others. The business equivalents of the dodoes, the dinosaurs, and the great ground sloths are in for a bad time—and they should be. It is fortunate for all of us that there was no Federal Biological Commission around when the first small furry mammals appeared and began eating dinosaur eggs. The commission would undoubtedly have perceived a "competitive advantage," labeled it an "unfair method of evolution," and stopped the whole process right there.

It is important to try to understand why this anticompetitive strain has developed in antitrust. The institutions primarily responsible are the Supreme Court, the enforcement agencies, and Congress.

The Root of the FTC's Confusion

HAROLD B. MEYERS

Harold B. Meyers writes regularly on the relations between government and business for *Fortune*.

AT THE main entrances of the Federal Trade Commission building in Washington stand two massive granite dray horses, seventeen feet long and fifteen feet tall. Each horse is held back from murderous charge by a stalwart, bare-chested workman. Ever since the designs were chosen in 1938 there has been disagreement over just what is going on. "The sculpture is nonsymbolic," said the selection committee of art experts. Sculptor Michael Lantz disagreed. He saw something quite specific in his statues. "They are the symbol of the ability of man to govern tremendous power," Lantz declared. "The theory behind the design is that man controls trade. Trade is an enormous thing, like the horse in the design. But man by his intelligence controls the horse, as he controls trade."

However symbolic the taming of the horses really is, the confusion over their meaning is uncannily appropriate to the Federal Trade Commission. Uncertainty over what it should be and how it should perform its functions was present at the agency's birth in 1914, and the fog has never quite been dispelled. Established to celebrate and protect the benefits of free competition, the FTC has often seemed to view competition as desirable only if it could be had without losers—or winners. The FTC has been irrelevant to many of the dramatic economic changes that have occurred in its lifetime. It has been as much of a nuisance as an aid to business, especially small business. Nor has it been a particularly effective white knight in protecting the basic interests of consumers.

Valuable as it has sometimes been as a Socratic gadfly, asking questions about the economy that needed to be asked, the FTC has still failed to lay down the clear rules of the road that businessmen need from government. Further, the FTC often seems to be doing work that could just as well be left to other agencies, such as the Department of Justice's Antitrust Division. Some of the FTC's work even seems to contradict antitrust, in the sense that instead of promoting competition it penalizes price cutting.

The agency's confusions and defects trace back to the legislative intent of the statutes granting the FTC much too broad discretionary authority. In passing the Sherman Act in 1890, Congress declared war against "restraint of trade" and monopoly. By 1914 it was felt that something more was needed; enforcement of the antitrust law through the courts had proved both slow and difficult. Congress therefore passed the Clayton Act amending the Sherman Act and, for good measure, created the FTC to be competition's special guardian. Its charter gave the FTC power to delve into unfair methods of competition in commerce (including deceptive advertising) and to issue cease-and-desist orders against those practices it found to be against the public interest.

To this inclusive mandate Congress in 1936 added the Robinson-Patman Act. This law has been characterized by Washington antitrust lawyer Frederick M. Rowe as "a legal enigma whose mysteries are familiar to many but fathomed by few." In *Price Discrimination Under the Robinson-Patman Act,* Rowe calls the act an "anti-antitrust" measure and says it was a legacy of the same depression-bred faith in combination, rather than competition, that produced the ill-fated Blue Eagle of the National Recovery Administration. Though supposedly aimed at "big buyers," such as chain stores, which used volume purchasing to gain unjustified price advantages, Robinson-Patman has been invoked most often against small firms for relatively insignificant violations. Rowe, in fact, proposed a Parkinson's law of FTC enforcement: "That Robinson-Patman proceedings proliferate with the ease of making a case."

This statutory underpinning gives the FTC more than enough to do—even with its $11,473,000 budget and 1,150 employees. And indeed, lack of activity has never been one of the agency's faults. In fiscal 1962 the FTC received 5,519 complaints involving deceptive practices and another 1,451 charging restraints of trade. Most of these complaints, it is important to note, were made by disadvantaged competitors; businessmen use the FTC as well as condemn it. The commission completed 1,677 investigations in 1962, approved 474 complaints, and issued 407 cease-and-desist orders (356 of them uncontested consent decrees).

The trouble is that amidst all this frenetic activity it is difficult to find a clear policy line on which businessmen can act. Consider the following.

DECEPTIVE PRACTICES

In 1960 the FTC issued a complaint against the Quaker Oats Company on the grounds that it misrepresented briquets as "charcoal" when they were actually made principally from the residue of corncobs. Quaker Oats fought back, arguing that there was no misrepresentation in calling its product "Chuck Wagon Charcoal Briquets." The FTC examiner who first heard the case agreed, citing evidence that nine dictionaries failed to limit "charcoal" to mean only the charred residue of wood. "In the face of these definitions," said the examiner, "it is difficult to see how a finding could properly be made that charcoal, even when restricted to fuel charcoal, can be made from no material other than wood, or that such is the understanding of the public." The FTC staff appealed the findings, and oral arguments were heard by the full commission. However, such a case seems hardly worth the time and money it has consumed. If charcoal means what the dictionary says, there was no misrepresentation, and if the product burned as well as wood charcoal and was not harmful, why should the government be concerned?

DISCRIMINATORY PROMOTIONAL ALLOWANCES

J. A. Folger Company of Kansas City, second-largest coffee manufacturer in the nation, took part in "Foodaramas" sponsored in 1958 and 1959 by the Benner Tea Company, a small retail grocery chain with headquarters in Burlington, Iowa. The Foodaramas were open-house affairs at which samples of food were given away, but no sales were made. Folger paid Benner $150 each year for booths in which to promote its Folger brand. Other Folger customers, competing with Benner, protested to the FTC. The FTC brought a complaint against Folger under the Robinson-Patman Act, charging that Folger had failed to offer these other customers proportionally equal promotional allowances. Deciding the case the FTC said in its majority opinion: "It is this type of favoritism to a customer such as a chain organization, even in relatively small individual contributions, which the law exactly proscribes." Folger was ordered to stop discriminating among competing customers in paying promotional allowances— under all circumstances, not just at food fairs. In a minority opinion, Commissioner Philip Elman argued that the order against Folger was far too broad and should have been issued, if at all, only against the kind of food-fair activity complained of. Said Elman crisply: "If there were any violations here, they were marginal, isolated, and in an uncertain area of the law."

ANTICOMPETITIVE AND MONOPOLISTIC PRACTICES, MERGERS

Luria Brothers Inc. of Philadelphia, largest iron and steel scrap dealer in the United States, was charged by the FTC in 1954 with engaging in illegal and competition-damaging practices with a group of major United States and foreign steel producers. Luria and the mills, said the FTC, had entered into agreements whereby Luria became the principal source of scrap for them. The company increased its share of total United States scrap sales from 17.1 percent to 33.7 percent while its share of sales to the cited mills rose from 35.9 percent in 1947 to 78.5 percent in 1954. These "full supply arrangements" gave Luria the power to control prices received by other brokers and dealers, the FTC alleged, and the company reinforced its position by acquiring competing firms in at least two instances. Some 250 witnesses testified during 113 days of hearings, producing a transcript of more than 14,000 pages and introducing more than 1,300 exhibits. Nine years after the complaint was issued, the FTC concluded that the charges had been generally sustained. It issued an order against Luria and the steel producers, including Bethlehem, U.S. Steel, National Steel, and ten others. The order provided, among other things, that the cited mills must buy at least 50 percent of their annual scrap requirements from suppliers other than Luria for the next five years, so long as the other suppliers are competitive in price and quality. Luria was also told to divest itself of one competing scrap company it acquired in 1950; it cannot buy out any more dealers for five years without prior FTC approval.

The best criticism of the FTC's majority decision, which Luria has appealed, came in another thoughtful dissent by Commissioner Elman. He argued that it had not been shown that there was anything unlawful about the "exclusive patronage of Luria by each of the mill respondents." He added that the case "has little relevance to present conditions in the scrap market"—which, in the last decade, has changed from a sellers' to a buyers' market. A more useful proceeding, Elman suggested, would be a current investigation "to determine what corrective administrative action, if any, is required to maintain or re-establish healthy competition" in the scrap industry as it exists today. In effect, he accused his fellow commissioners of blindly beating a dead horse.

DISCRIMINATORY PRICING

The Borden Company has been selling evaporated milk under its own well-known brand since 1892. About 1938 it entered the business of packing evaporated milk for sale under the private labels of purchasers. This private-label milk was sold at prices "consistently and substantially" lower than Borden-label milk of like grade and quality. The company justified the discrepancy in price on the grounds that its brand name, diligently promoted over many years, added to the salability, and hence the value, of the product. Smaller competitors, however, thought the lower price for private-label stock was intended to draw away their customers and drive them out of business, thus increasing Borden's already large share of the milk-packing market. At their behest, the FTC charged Borden in 1958 with a Robinson-Patman violation—unlawful price discrimination tending to lessen competition substantially. A hearing examiner filed an initial decision dismissing the complaint, but the commission reversed his finding and ordered Borden to cease discriminating in the price of *any* of its food products. Borden has appealed.

In reaching this decision, the commission (with Elman dissenting and two other members not participating) concluded that private-label buyers—generally larger retailers and chains—were given an unfair adavntage over retailers that did not have enough volume to justify establishing their own brands. "The testimony from wholesalers as well as retailers disclosed the extremely low or nonexistent profit margins on evaporated milk," Chairman Dixon wrote, noting also that private-label milk was used as a loss leader to attract customers. Borden's actions, therefore, were found offensive by the FTC in two ways: (1) Small evaporated-milk producers were driven to the wall by Borden's competition, and this competition threatened the competitive situation in the industry; (2) the low prices forced on all private-label producers put a squeeze on wholesalers and retailers that were too small to have their own brands and were thus forced to stock the higher-priced brands. Nothing was said about possible benefit to consumers from the bitter competition in canned milk.

These cases—from *Quaker Oats* to *Borden*—suggest the FTC's extraordinary range of powers and problems. Nelson Gaskill, who served as a commissioner from 1920 to 1925, once wrote, in words that hold true today: "So far as I could learn, at no time during the Commission's existence prior to my appearance and certainly never during the five years of my service were there even the beginnings of a definite policy or the shadow of an established specific field of jurisdiction. . . . At least one result of this policy of no policy was that everything conceivable was tried at least once."

The "policy of no policy" still plagues the FTC, and the trouble is compounded by the fluctuating winds of politics. Even the staff is subject to rapid turnover and cronyism. In the Eisenhower Administration most of the principal staff directors were Republicans. Today, though the FTC claims to be a "bipartisan" agency, the six major bureaus are all headed by Democrats and no more than two of the twenty lesser divisions are directed by a Republican. Meanwhile the commissioners at the top come and go, and few bother to serve out their appointed seven-year term. At any point of time, the commission resembles a Congress more than a court, with its own built-in majority and minorities.

Taxes and Controls

MARRINER ECCLES

Marriner Eccles was Chairman of the Federal Reserve Board from 1936 to 1948. This article is from his book, Beckoning Frontiers, *published in 1951.*

THE WINTER and spring of disasters on the fighting front following Pearl Harbor seemed to be duplicated in part on the domestic front. Here, too, there was drift. By the first part of 1942 all the signs of inflation were clearly visible, yet an integrated program to deal with them had not yet been formed.

The President was taxed to the limit of human endurance in attending to the immediate military tasks that faced the nation. The Congress had its attention drawn to the elections in November. The various parts of the economic community felt the heady wine of "prosperity" for the first time in thirteen years. Each group in its own way—businessmen, laborers, and farmers—was strongly tempted to drink more of the stuff that had been denied it for so long. Each group was prepared to have prohibitive rules clamped down on other groups, but not on itself. All that could be done to stem the inflationary tide was a series of stopgap measures that were splintered almost as soon as they were put in place. . . .

While there were many of us in Washington who were deeply involved in this question, I believe it was a series of conferences Harold Smith, the Director of the Budget, had with Leon Henderson and myself that brought matters to a head. With Smith acting as our friend at court, the President on March 17, 1942 was at last induced to order basic staff and command work on the problem of inflation. On that day he directed Vice President Henry Wallace, Secretary of the Treasury Henry Morgenthau, Price Administrator Leon Henderson, Secretary of Agriculture Claude Wickard, and myself to draft a coordinated anti-inflationary program.

The vicious circle with which we had to deal was aptly described in a Bureau of the Budget memorandum sent to the

President on March 26. It pointed out that inflation could not be stopped as long as wage increases as well as rising governmental expenditures created additional purchasing power. Wage increases could not be stopped as long as prices rose. Price rises could not be stopped unless part of the rapidly increasing purchasing power was absorbed by fiscal measures. Fiscal measures could not be effective as long as businessmen, wage-earners, and farmers could make up for taxes by increasing their incomes.

Morgenthau, who knew the trend of our thinking, held himself aloof from the joint effort. He was, I believe, somewhat piqued that as Secretary of the Treasury he was not made head of the committee, but was placed on an equal footing with others, and particularly with Harold Smith. But the rest of us met off and on for a month to do what the President directed. With the help of Dr. Alvin H. Hansen and Dr. Gerhard Colm, who were brought in for technical assistance, the draft program was completed and then submitted to the President on April 18. Morgenthau did not sign it. He was against any lowering of income-tax exemptions and a freezing of wages, both of which were basic to any inflationary-control program.

The remainder of the committee reported to the President that we had examined the possibilities of a partial program to check inflation under an all-out war effort, but we had come to the conclusion "that partial programs will not work and that only a simultaneous attack on prices, rents, wages, profits, and mass purchasing power will suffice. Every element is essential to the effectiveness of every other element. Any lesser program must fail." Such a comprehensive program, we added, not only was economically and politically sound, but would be strongly backed by the public.

As for *price control:* we urged that rents should be stabilized within the limits of the Emergency Price Control Act; that a ceiling be placed immediately on all prices—retail, wholesale, and manufacturing. The proposed general ceiling would include most foods and all clothing at retail. To do this, the Emergency Price Control Act would have to be stretched. If the cost of living was to be fully stabilized, the 110-per-cent parity limitation had to be stricken from the price law. At the same time we recommended that the existing restrictions on the sale of government-held commodities be removed.

As for the *wage control:* we proposed the proclamation of a policy of stabilizing wage rates except those below forty cents per hour. The hope had often been expressed that stabilization of the cost of living would be enough and that the stabilization of wage rates would be unnecessary, but this hope was unfounded. Wage *income* was certain to rise even if wage *rates* were stabilized. The number of employed workers in a family of workers would continue to rise. Furthermore, employees would work more hours per week at overtime premiums and they would move up continually from lower- to higher-paid jobs. "Stabilization of wage rates," we said, "eliminates only one important inflationary factor. It reduces the excess of purchasing power over shortened supply so that the remainder of the problem can be managed through fiscal and price-control measures. Unless wage rates are controlled, we believe that increased labor costs and increased consumer demand will shatter the price ceiling and thereby discredit price administration and Government in general."

We asked that a standard work week of forty-eight hours should be proclaimed with time-and-a-half paid for overtime above forty hours, that double time for Sundays and holidays should be abandoned, and that restrictive labor practices should be eliminated.

As for *profits:* we noted that some salaries and bonuses of management had been raised out of all reason. These instances were well known to labor and farmers and incited demands for higher wages and higher farm prices. While the proposals for profit taxation in a Treasury bill then pending would reduce 1942 profits at the disposal of corporations below the 1941 level, even these stiff tax proposals would permit some corporations and some individuals to retain unreasonable gains.

To remedy this we proposed three steps: that excess-profit tax provisions of pending Treasury proposals should be tightened; that unreasonable salaries and bonuses, and salaries and bonuses that had been increased to avoid corporate taxation, should be eliminated by strict application of the internal-revenue laws that prohibit deductions of "unreasonable" salaries in computing net income; that a ceiling of fifty thousand dollars after taxes should be placed on individual incomes, thereby dramatizing the equality of sacrifice implicit in the proposed over-all program.

As for *mass purchasing power:* we informed the President that price and wage stabilization was doomed to failure unless the explosive pressure of excess purchasing power was reduced through appropriate tax and savings measures.

The pending tax bill of the Treasury, we said, fell far short of that requirement, for even if wage rates were stabilized and the complete. Treasury tax program was enacted immediately, excess purchasing power in 1942 would amount to more than $10 billion. Furthermore, much of the excess would be in the hands of the people who typically spend almost all of their income—an income not materially affected by the income tax. What we needed was a tax system that would absorb purchasing power at the annual rate of $6 billion during the first half of the fiscal year 1943, and above $10 billion for the second half.

As for the Treasury's voluntary-savings program, that too was hopelessly inadequate. Less than ten per cent of all savings bonds had been bought by individuals in the lower-income bracket. Over ninety per cent of the bonds sold merely represented the normal savings of middle- and higher-income groups. Thus a voluntary-savings program would not sufficiently curtail the consumption of the lower-income groups. To do the job, we strongly recommended that some type of compulsory universal saving should be adopted.

To further the same purpose behind a universal-savings plan, we suggested that Congress be requested to make a reduction of exemptions under the individual income tax. The exemptions suggested would be reduced to $500 for a single person, $1,000 for married people, and $250 for each dependent, with a moderate rate for the lowest-income bracket. This reduction, based on the then cost of living, we felt, would not add too great a burden on the individual brought under the income tax for the first time.

The President's committee considered at some length the role of consumption taxes in a war period, but decided against recommending them at that time. We believed that such measures as low-bracket income taxes, increased universal savings, and social security were superior to general sales taxes. We suggested, however, that the President might announce to the country and to Congress that he was determined to recommend a war consumption tax if the fiscal program we had suggested did not prove equal to absorbing the excess purchasing power. "The stabilization program," we said, "must be executed under all circumstances

—if necessary by resort to regressive forms of taxation, which are normally undesirable but more desirable than an inflationary price rise."

We recognized that Congress was likely to enact a sales tax with or without the President's request. But we suggested that if the President indicated that a war consumption tax might be necessary for future use, it might deter Congress at that time from enacting such a tax as a substitute for a portion of the income and profits taxes included in the Treasury bill then before Congress.

Finally, as an essential supplement to the balance of the program, we urged that credit expansion of all kinds had to be prevented or controlled.

This in broad outline was our plan of action. . . .

In his message to Congress on April 27, and in a subsequent Fireside Chat, the President did take notice of the imminence of inflation and called for action in seven areas. The ones he enumerated were drawn from the document we had submitted to him on April 18. Still, despite the eloquence of his chat, it was vague and general in its substance. In essence his program called on Congress to build a strong basement for prices, but gave no specific instructions on how the roof was to be tied down. Through this gap Congress looked up at the elements, saw the elections of November in the distance, and accordingly did very little. And so the inflationary spiral continued. . . .

In the ensuing months of congressional inactivity, we debated whether a further effort should be made by the President to bestir the Congress or whether he should stabilize prices by means of an executive order issued under his emergency powers.

By July 1942 the President's seven-point program issued in April was a complete shambles. All elements in the land were straining to free themselves from the seeming disadvantages they suffered in contrast with their neighbors. The "little-steel formula" invited some farm leaders to ask for bigger farm prices. A rise in the cost of living led some labor leaders to seek further wage increases—all this at a time when Congress wanted to get out of Washington and start campaigning.

It seemed for a time that Roosevelt would deal with the rising cost of living by means of an executive order. Robert Sherwood has related that the President's Labor Day address dealing with the problem of inflation was first written as a proclamation and explanation of such an order. The final decision was a compromise. Roosevelt sent Congress a demand for action by October 1, 1942, and coupled it with a clear warning that if Congress did not act, he would.

The message resulted in the enactment by Congress of the Stabilization Act, which Roosevelt signed on October 2. Among other things, it established an Office of Economic Stabilization, and Justice Byrnes stepped down from the Supreme Court to become the Director of that office. The powers given him to stabilize farm and wage prices were broad ones and represented a major step forward in providing the grappling-hooks with which prices could be bound to the earth. But the grant of these powers left open a wide area of disagreement on how they should be used and, in particular, how they should be used in regard to wage stabilization. The bulges and strains in the economy continued to disfigure the national scene.

In November 1942 I tried to point this out to the advisory committee that assisted Byrnes in his work. As I recall, the committee was formed of eight men, two each representing labor, agriculture, business, and the general public. At a meeting with this committee on November 13, I argued that if we were to control excess purchasing power and preserve reasonable economic stability, we had to resort to far more drastic measures to curtail civilian spending power than those adopted up to that time. At that time the expendable income had reached a point where it exceeded by $40 billion the value of the goods available for sale. Given the character of American saving and spending habits, we faced a prospect of a rise in the cost of living by at least a third, brought on by the pressure of the excess purchasing power on hand.

The extent to which we are failing to meet the problem on the domestic front, I continued, was illustrated by a comparison with the British and Canadian experience at that time. They were financing about one half of their expenditures by taxation and one half out of borrowing in contrast with our one quarter from taxation and three quarters from borrowing. Of the half they borrowed, about two thirds came from the general public and only one third from the inflationary process of bank borrowing. In contrast, of the part we borrowed, one third came from the general public and nearly two thirds from the banking system. How could we change this trend?

We all recognize the limitation of what price control and rationing can do by themselves [I said to the Advisory Committee]. The strongest administrative machinery would crumble under the pressure of the excessive purchasing power now flowing into the hands of the American public. A hard-boiled fiscal policy is our only hope of reducing the pressure enough to permit rationing to function.

On the fiscal front, I urged on the committee that the ratio of taxation to borrowing, as well as the ration between nonbank and bank borrowing, should be of the British and Canadian variety. While decreasing purchasing power in this way, there was the offsetting need to increase the supply of goods. There, too, we could learn much from our English friends. In Great Britain the average working week was about 54 hours for nonagricultural workers. In the United States it was only 43 hours. We needed to increase the work week to 48 hours. "Organized labor won the 40-hour week after many years of painful effort and struggle," I said. "It should be made unmistakably clear that the government does not propose to abolish but merely to suspend the legislation guaranteeing this achievement." In addition, federal action should be coupled with further action that would impose a blanket prohibition on working more than 60 hours a week except in grave emergencies.

Finally, I argued that we could release resources for essential use by employing existing training facilities in the colleges for the armed forces rather than to build new facilities destined for the scrap heap after the war. In this way we could economize the use of scarce building materials and labor. We could also release resources for essential use by cutting down on advertising. It seemed contradictory to me that at a time when it was the government's declared policy to curb civilian demand, advertising of all kinds continued to whet the public's appetite to buy. The government not only permitted this, but by various means actually encouraged this misuse of resources. First, in our tax laws we allowed generous deductions for advertising expenses, and thereby not only virtually paid for advertising out of the public treasury, but encouraged it when a company was subject to excess-profit taxes. Second, we continued to encourage appeals to the public that were wholly inconsistent with the government program of conserving civilian goods and making the most efficient use of our resources. A great deal of labor and scarce material were thus squandered, to say nothing of the additional burdens on transportation and postal facilities, which were already strained.

When I had finished this statement, Brynes commended it as being "courageous and interesting." Then he went around the table and called on each of the eight Board members to criticize or to associate himself with it. Not a person present spoke up for the program.

I admit it was a tough program and had no political appeal. Still, while others may have had good personal reasons for remaining silent, I could not do so.

I repeated this same argument before the Senate Banking and Currency Committee on February 17, 1943, and there declared that the government "was doing a very bad" job of war financing compared with other countries; that we needed higher taxes and less borrowing from the banks if we were to control inflation. Almost a month later, on March 30, before the Central States group of the Investment Bankers Association meeting in Chicago, I repeated this same argument and placed on Congress the responsibility for the inadequacy of our war financing.

Again this theme was repeated in a nation-wide broadcast on April 14 while the Treasury's second war-loan drive was on to raise $13 billion through the sale of war bonds. I said at that time:

The question is not whether the goal of this campaign will be reached, but how it is reached. The government can always raise the money it needs. What is of vital importance to every man, woman, and child in the country is that the money needed to wage this war is raised in a way that will not result in a disastrous rise in the cost of living. This means it must be financed out of savings and not by additional bank money.

The heavy oversubscription in the drive induced many people to argue that there was no further need for stiffer taxes. What they ignored was the way Treasury offerings found their way ultimately into the banks, with inflationary consequences that have been detailed already. They also ignored the fact that the Treasury's offering absorbed only a fraction of the $55-billion purchasing power that was then on hand in excess of the amount of consumer goods available.

In the course of testimony before the House Banking and Currency Committee on May 13, 1943, I argued for a separation of individual and bank borrowing when the special drives for bond sales are put on; the effort, I said, should be centered on getting individuals to buy. If this was done, then an estimated $15 to $20 billion more bonds might be purchased by individuals in the new loan drives. But, even so, this would leave upwards of $25 billion in excess purchasing power that had to be absorbed by taxes. More taxes and still more taxes were the only solution if we were to curb inflation. I flatly denied that the success of the Treasury's drive in any way reduced the necessity for a comprehensive tax program.

The whole of this testimony, added to what had gone before it, resulted in an increase in tension between Secretary Morgenthau and me. It was heightened by Morgenthau's "take-it-or-leave-it" speech to the Board of Governors and Reserve Bank presidents which he made at that time. But, like all other differences, this one was also composed, and it was agreed that in the future the offerings to the public would be separated from offerings to the banks; that the emphasis be put on individual purchases as a means of curbing inflation. Still, this agreement did not end the need for additional tax revenues to siphon off the excess purchasing power over and above that would be absorbed by increasing individual purchases of securities.

Accordingly I continued to press for additional taxes and a compulsory savings program. In October 1943 the House Ways and Means Committee was considering a new tax bill recommended by the Treasury calling for $10.5 billion in additional revenues. When I appeared before the committee in connection with this bill, I urged an even higher tax figure of $13 billion. Not only was the proposal I made promptly rejected, but even the Treasury proposal was largely scrapped. Indicative of congressional attitudes at that time relative to increasing taxes, Chairman Robert L. Doughton of the House Ways and Means Committee had this to say about my suggested revision of the tax bill:

"Amazing, fantastic, and visionary. I don't like it at all. If possible, it is worse than the Treasury program."

In his budget message of 1944 President Roosevelt asked that taxes be stepped up to get an additional $10 billion; the request was based on the fact that despite earlier tax hikes the public was still left with a considerable sum of money with which it could increase inflationary pressures. Harold W. Smith, Leon Henderson, and I strongly urged the President to take the course of action reflected in his message. Had the Congress been of a similar mind, there is no question that subsequent inflation might have been mitigated. Congress, however, remained committed to easy financial devices and in the election year of 1944 prepared to have the war financed by bank credit rather than by stiffer taxes. The result was a tax bill that Roosevelt vetoed in language so sharp that it provoked Senator Alben Barkley to resign as majority leader of the Senate. He was induced, however, to resume his post and Congress promptly proceeded to override the President's veto. The action may have satisfied those who saw in it a reassertion of legislative leadership by Congress in the face of attempted encroachments by the executive. But, to be truly praiseworthy, the independence of the legislature should have been asserted on behalf of sound public policy. In this case, the legislature was wrong and the executive was right, and we all were to suffer because the legislature's point of view prevailed.

Ultimately a good part of the legislation that was required to fight an all-out war finally was written into law. Cumulative figures on the fiscal front showed that of $380 billion raised by the government between June 30, 1940 and the end of 1945, $153 billion came from taxes, or about 40 per cent. The remainder, $228 billion, or about 60 per cent, was raised by borrowing. Of the total borrowed, $133 billion, or about 60 per cent, came from selling government securities to investors other than commercial banks and the Federal Reserve banks. Approximately $95 billion, or 40 per cent, of the amount borrowed was raised by selling government securities to the commercial banking system. By the end of the war the percentage figures of taxes in relation to borrowing, and of borrowing from banks and nonbank investors, had improved considerably over what they were when I appeared before the Byrnes committee in November 1942, but the improvement was not enough to spare us from a postwar hangover.

The Civil Aeronautics Board Answers a House Committee

The Subcommittee on Legislative Oversight of the House Committee on Interstate and Foreign Commerce sent a formal questionnaire to the Civil Aeronautics Board in 1957. The CAB answered in 1960. Some of the questions posed by the Committee and the CAB responses are given here.

●

WHAT CONTACTS AND CHANNELS OF COMMUNICATION, FORMAL AND INFORMAL, ARE THERE BETWEEN THE CIVIL AERONAUTICS BOARD AND THOSE REGULATED? In formal cases involving quasi-judicial functions, the parties file briefs, motions, answers and other pleadings with the Board, copies of which are delivered. In addition, representatives of airlines, air freight forwarders, pilot and aircraft organizations, other business concerns having a legitimate interest in the particular proceeding, travel agents, cities and chambers of commerce appear before the Board in scheduled oral arguments.

In matters of an informal nature involving the Board's quasi-legislative and administrative functions, these parties may present their views to the Board on general industry problems, international negotiations, proposed amendments to the economic and safety rules and like matters. The industry also communicates with the Board by letter on similar matters or by informal visits.

There are also contacts with representatives of the regulated industry at conventions or conferences concerned with aeronautical or legal matters, at civic or ceremonial functions of a promotional nature, on inspection tours of industry facilities, and at related social affairs.

BETWEEN THE CAB STAFF AND THOSE REGULATED?

Bureau of Safety • The Director has been empowered by the Board to issue notices of proposed rule-making directly to the industry in anticipation of rule changes to be acted on by the Board. The staff is permitted to request the services of industry personnel in accident investigations. In such investigations, hearings are often held which are presided over by a Board member or staff member. Otherwise, communication between staff and those regulated is routine and includes the normal channels of communication such as correspondence and meetings.

Bureau of Air Operations • In the processing of economic cases involving hearing (e.g., route cases, rate cases and merger cases) numerous formal contacts and formal channels of communication exist. Personal contact and communication are had in prehearing conferences, mail rate conferences, hearings and oral arguments. These contacts are between staff assigned to the cases and/or their supervisors, on the one hand, and air carrier counsel, officials and staff on the other. Such contact and communication are also had in writing by means of exchange of requests for evidence, proposed statements of issues, statements of staff position, briefs to examiners, briefs to the Board, letters relating to procedural matters, letters supplying material for the record, and any other correspondence required by the formal processing of the proceeding.

In matters which may be handled without hearing (e.g., exemption applications, interlocking directorships, nonstop notices, and service suspension applications) written communication exists between staff of the Board and/or their supervisors, on the one hand, and air carrier counsel, officials and staff on the other. These communications are made to obtain information necessary for the processing of the particular matter; to advise on procedural requirements; to advise on substantive matters within the scope of the staff's authority; to reject tariff filings because of technical inadequacies; or for other reasons dictated by the requirements of the work. These communications are generally written over the signature of the Section Chief, Division Chief, Associate Bureau Director, or Bureau Director, according to the nature of the matter.

In the area of international civil air relations the airlines individually, and collectively through their associations, are regularly requested to comment on appropriate problems. This is accomplished through meetings with the Board, staff conferences, by letters and by personal and telephonic interview.

Other formal contact exists with carrier personnel through staff representation on Governmental committees where there is representation also by carriers or carrier associations. These include, principally, components of the Air Coordinating Committee and the Industry Advisory Committee on Aviation Mobilization.

Informal contacts and channels of communication exist between the staff and/or their supervisors, on the one hand, and air carrier counsel, officials and staff on the other, in hearing and nonhearing matters. These contacts usually are for the purpose of obtaining information needed by the Government in pending matters, to clarify exhibit material, to exchange views as to procedural dates, or for other purposes for which formal communication is not required in the handling of the particular item.

In connection with all of the above, it should be noted that the Board's regulations specifically provide that "in cases to be determined after notice and hearing and upon a record . . . it is improper that there be any private communication on the merits of the case to a member of the Board or its staff or to the examiner in the case by any person, either in private or public life, unless provided for by law."

Bureau of Hearing Examiners • Contact with those regulated is limited to the formal communications of the hearing process, plus communications on related matters similar to the communications which may occur between a judge and counsel for litigants.

Office of Administration • All carriers receiving subsidy submit monthly billings to the Carrier Payments Section, Office of Secretary and Comptroller. The processing of such billings frequently involves correspondence and conferences between staff members of the Board and the carrier or carriers involved.

Office of Carrier Accounts and Statistics • Formal channels of communication with the industry are effected through the issuance of accounting regulation, interpretations and waivers under delegated authority and the transmittal by mail to each Chief Accounting Officer of the individual carriers of copies of regulations, interpretations or waivers.

Informal communications are effected through telephone, letter, or personal visits in connection with the field or desk audit activities and in resolving particular accounting and/or reporting controversies. Informal oral and written communications with the industry are also effected through the Air Transport Association or the Independent Airlines Association, as applicable, in arranging for industry-wide contribution in resolving accounting and statistical problems.

Office of Compliance • The Office of Compliance has frequent occasion to contact those regulated. Such contacts are made by telephone, telegraph, letter and in person. Such contacts most frequently occur in the course of investigation or in the course of enforcement proceedings or litigation. Compliance attorneys must frequently consult with counsel for the regulated in drafting stipulations, in Board and Court proceedings, in issuing letters of reprimand, arriving at compromises, etc.

Office of the General Counsel • The General Counsel is the chief legal officer of the Board. It is the practice of his office to supply legal information to outside interested persons to the extent that this can be done consistently with other duties and within the proprieties applicable to rendering such information. These persons include not only airline representatives but airline passengers, shippers, government officials, legislators, and members of the public who may be affected in one way or another by the Act or the actions of the Board. Most of the inquiries are oral rather than written, and come from airline lawyers. The range of the inquiries is as wide as the field of regulation and their quality varies from the routine and simple to the very unusual and complex. The Office makes every attempt to be helpful within the bounds of the quasi-judicial and legislative proprieties of the Board's work and available staff. In rendering advice, no distinction is made between certificated and non-certificated airlines, or on any other basis of operating authority, or service or personalities. Every effort is made to avoid involvement in economic policy, the advice being limited to matters of law.

Office of Information • As part of its duty the Office informs industry representatives, orally and in writing, of actions and policies of the Board.

DO SUCH CHANNELS REACH ALL SEGMENTS OF THE INDUSTRY? Yes, formal and informal communications channels are open to all segments of the industry.

ARE THE CHANNELS AVAILABLE, FOR EXAMPLE, TO REPRESENTATIVES OF NON-SCHEDULED AIRLINES EQUIVALENT TO THOSE OF THE CERTIFICATED INDUSTRY? Yes.

WHAT INDUSTRY REPRESENTATIVES ARE IN FAIRLY CONSTANT LIAISON WITH THE AGENCY? WHAT ARE THEIR FUNCTIONS? Attorneys, of course, represent their clients in all legal matters before or involving the Board. Industry tariff experts, treasurers, controllers, economists and other officers and employees communicate with the agency at all levels.

All liaison or contacts between industry and the agency on quasi-judicial matters, of course, are accomplished through formal channels consistent with the Board's official code of ethical conduct, as well as with statutory, procedural requisites. Other communications on quasi-legislative and administrative matters do not require the same formality.

IN WHAT INSTANCES DOES THE LAW PROVIDE FOR AGENCY RATIFICATION OF INDUSTRY REGULATORY ACTION? Technically speaking, the law neither provides for "regulatory action" by the industry nor for "agency ratification" thereof. Section 412 of the Act contemplates that a great variety of cooperative agreements affecting air transportation will be entered into between carriers, but provides that all such agreements must be submitted to the Board for approval or disapproval to guard against their being in contravention of the Act or the public interest. In a non-technical and rather loose sense, it might be said that such agreements attempt to "regulate" and subsequent Board approval constitutes a "ratification."

TO WHAT EXTENT, IF ANY, IS AGENCY POLICY IN PRACTICE MADE BY THE REGULATED INDUSTRY, WITH THE AGENCY PROVIDING DE FACTO RATIFICATION? In a strict sense, the answer is *to no extent*. There is, however, a broader aspect to this problem which, in the economic area of the Board's regulatory powers, stems from the underlying philosophy of public utility regulation that a regulatory agency is not the manager of a utility. Once the basic operating authority is granted, it is an airline's privilege and responsibility in the first instance to run the show within the legal boundaries set out in the legislation governing it. The regulatory agency's essential responsibility is to provide the climate for healthy growth and service called for by the legislation and to correct any abuses that might develop. A good example of this is section 408 of the Civil Aeronautics Act of 1938 dealing with various agreements relating to acquisition of control by one airline of an other, which require approval by the Board. The Act does not impose any duty to enter into any such agreements. The initiative is with the airlines, with the Board exercising a veto power in the public interest.

An even better example of this general philosophy is section 404 of the Act which places the responsibility upon airlines to establish lawful passenger and property rates and furnish adequate service. The Board does not establish such rates and service practices in the first instance, but is given the authority in section 1002 to correct rates and service practices which do not conform to the standards of the Act. In like manner, the responsibility for honest, efficient and economical operations is upon an airline. The Board does not manage the airline, nor does it tell its manager how to manage. But if the airline should be mismanaged and incur losses thereby, for example, the Board will refuse to consider such losses in fixing commercial rates or awarding subsidy under section 406.

ARE ANY INSTANCES AVAILABLE TO SHOW PRESSURES, DIRECT OR INDIRECT, BY THE REGULATED INDUSTRY, OR PART OF IT, UPON THE AGENCY IN

(a) FORMULATION OF RULES AND REGULATIONS?
(b) FORMULATION OF AGENCY POLICIES?
(c) DECISION OF SPECIFIC CASES?
(d) CONDUCT OF INVESTIGATIONS?

There have been occasions when the Board was made aware of attempts on the part of various members of the regulated industry to bring pressure to bear upon the Board in an effort to obtain, by means other than the facts of a formal record, favorable action in pending proceedings. The instances involved small as well as large carriers, and scheduled as well as non-scheduled carriers. Competition for routes sometimes becomes frenzied and it is in this type of proceeding where the greatest abuse of the Board's processes have been encountered in the past. The methods of the carriers involved were indirect, in that they would ask stockholders, employees, local and federal government officials and influential businessmen to urge the Board to decide the pending case in favor of the carrier involved, and many such communications have been addressed to the Board outside of the formal record.

An example of indirect pressure can be found in connection

with the Board's current General Passenger Fare Investigation. This proceeding has not been the subject of wide news coverage but at the same time it has been the subject of considerable editorial comment. Particularly during the winter of 1957–58, editorials appeared in a large segment of the daily press containing a similarity of statistical references, urging the Board to provide financial relief to the air transport industry through higher passenger fares. While the Board made no official judgment as to the source of this editorial campaign, it did make clear that it would not be influenced by or accept the validity of the published material. On March 20, 1958, the Board stated publicly:

"We have, of course, regretted the statements in the press and in trade publications which to us seemed to give an inaccurate and incomplete picture of the general passenger fare investigation and of the Board's attitude toward passenger fare increases. However, we believe as a basic principle of democracy that the right of the press to comment freely on all public affairs is one of the surest and strongest forces for good government."

It will be recognized that it is not always easy to discover a deliberate attempt to so influence, and it must also be considered that where quasi-legislative matters are involved the area of permissible "fair comment" is perhaps broader than in purely quasi-judicial matters. Nevertheless, in several instances where there appeared little doubt of the impropriety of a carrier's action, the Board sent a reprimand and warned that more drastic action would follow in case of repetition. The Board has also appealed to the air carrier associations to aid in curbing such abuses in the future. In connection with this question, we call attention to the following provisions of the Board's Rules of Practice:

"300.2 Hearing Cases—Improper Influence. It is essential in cases to be determined after notice and hearing and upon a record that the Board's judicial character be recognized and protected.
*   *   *
"(c) It is improper that there be any effort by any person interested in the case to sway the judgment of the Board by attempting to bring pressure or influence to bear upon the members of the Board or its staff, or that such person or any member of the Board's staff, directly or indirectly, give statements to the press or radio, by paid advertisements or otherwise, designed to influence the Board's judgment in the case."

PART FOUR   Techniques of Manipulation

The Steel-price Controversy, 1962

*On April 11, 1962 President Kennedy took a firm stand against
across-the-board increases in the price of steel announced first by
United States Steel and then, in rapid succession, by the other
major steel producers. Grant McConnell, Professor of Political
Science at the University of Chicago, here discusses the aftermath
of that encounter and analyzes the techniques used by the President to force the steel companies to rescind the price increase.*

WHEN THE 5:44 left Grand Central Station on the evening of
Monday, April 16, 1962, the first stunning effects of U.S. Steel's
defeat had passed. Advertising executives, vice-presidents, and
presidents of companies in a variety of fields, their conclusions
hardened by conversation with associates through the day and
their intuitions sharpened over after-work martinis, talked in bitter and apprehensive tones of what the now clouded future must
hold for business. Within the thirty-six minutes that the Central's schedule allows for the run to Scarsdale it was clear that
there was a great upwelling of feeling within the business community. And it was not just on the train to Scarsdale that this
was apparent. It could have been seen and heard and felt on cars
that were rolling or about to roll to Paoli, to Wilmette, to Bur-
lingame.

Although the reaction of business was, after the initial shock,
swift and sure, there was a curious period in which opinion in
other segments of the nation was less certain and less compre-
hending. There were many signs of this disorientation. A number
of reliable observers have said that the private reaction of most
senators and congressmen, regardless of party was pleasure in the
humiliation of Big Steel. This observation may have been exag-
gerated. Moreover, in so far as it was accurate, it may have

reflected the professional bias of politicians whatever their affiliations. . . .

Editorial writers and ordinary citizens alike denounced the captains of the steel industry and rejoiced in their comeuppance. It was a sign, perhaps, of that latent Populism which occasionally bursts to the surface and sweeps across the nation. Sometimes these outbursts are short and sometimes they are long, but this one was short. Nevertheless, as late as early June there was evidence that the spasm was not entirely over. Walter Lippmann, speaking then on television, said that the price increase by United States Steel was a direct challenge to the President and that it put him in a position where he had to act.

There were even businessmen who were willing to defend the actions that President Kennedy had taken. Thus, in mid-May Mr. Ernest Henderson, President of the Sheraton Corporation of America, remarked, "It would seem that the steel company, by taking advantage of the government's intervention in the wage negotiations, was at least by implication accepting the principle of a noninflationary settlement. Yet the almost immediate raising of prices could hardly have been called noninflationary. President Kennedy, knowing that labor had been talked into swallowing a quite bitter pill in order to prevent an upward price spiral, could hardly have been expected to react calmly on hearing that, despite the relatively reasonable attitude of labor, steel prices went up anyway."

Viewpoints such as these, however, did not make up the whole of American public opinion, at least for long. Governor Rockefeller of New York was more thoughtful. He remarked that the affair of steel was "very sad." Senator Barry Goldwater, who had been reared in the crystalline air of Arizona, said with forthright clarity that the Kennedy administration was trying to "socialize the business of the country." "When we have a President who takes it upon himself to set prices in this country, then I suggest that every man, woman and child knows what we are up against. We need no longer hold back and be careful about what we say about our opposition."

If the outpourings that shortly followed Mr. Goldwater's statement are evidence, a major portion of the business community had been listening and took his advice with utter seriousness. Gradually at first, and then with a great torrent after the *New*

York Times printed the comment about businessmen which President Kennedy was supposed to have uttered on the night of [U.S. Steel president] Roger Blough's visit to the White House on April 10, the business press and then the daily press became filled with bitter recriminations against the President. It was a phenomenon with few precedents. On a small scale it had been duplicated by the tirades which had been loosed on President Truman. He, also, had once uttered a term of abuse about an opponent of the moment, but that opponent was a music critic and thus a figure of less importance to the nation than businessmen. Mr. Truman had also tangled with the steel industry, but for this he had been forgiven, since, unlike Mr. Kennedy, he had lost. For a genuine analogy it was necessary to go back to the days of Franklin D. Roosevelt. And this was very close to the heart of the matter. The language, the imagery, even the jokes of the months of April, May, June, and July, 1962, were those of the later nineteen-thirties, and the target was the same, the President, indeed, perhaps the same President.

The attacks upon Mr. Kennedy were of such an intensity and such a volume that he very soon found it necessary to issue public and vociferous denials that he was "anti-business." Neither these denials nor the partial reconciliation that was arranged between him and Mr. Blough had any effect upon the tide of hysteria which was running within the business community. Inescapably, the force of this hysteria spread. A Gallup Poll in early April, taken before the crisis in steel, showed that the President had the approval of 77 per cent of those questioned for their opinion of the manner in which he had been handling his job. In May, several weeks after the crisis, that figure dropped to a meager 73 per cent. This was despite the initial wave of popular enthusiasm for Mr. Kennedy's mastery of the crisis.

Through the weeks of May prophecies of disaster came in with increasing frequency and vehemence. Perhaps the central item in these dark forebodings was that a climate of fear had been created by the President's awesome "display of naked political power." The President had destroyed that noblest of business traits, confidence. As the stories and the humors were exchanged on commuter trains and wherever business leaders met with their own kind, insulated against the views of outsiders, the sense of doom mounted among the decision makers of the business world.

The prophets' words came true on May 28. This was Black Monday in the stock market. On this day there occurred the largest one-day dollar loss in the history of the New York Stock Exchange, more than 20 billion dollars. It was a disaster which the first commentators could liken only to the great crash of '29. That time, it was true, was really worse in its impact, but who now, any more than at the first inkling of disaster then, could tell how far the effects might go? It was not as bad, it could not be as bad. But there was this fact: a vastly greater number of Americans—perhaps some 17 million of them—this time were shareholders in the great firms of American business whose names were listed upon the exchanges.

The market made a quick and striking recovery within a very short time, but the evidence was in to show, no few business spokesmen proclaimed, that the actions of President Kennedy in the affair of steel had cost the nation dearly. The damage was already incalculable, and what it might mean for the future of the economy no one could safely tell. The condition of the nation's economic health suddenly became the object of almost universal concern. The words of the professional economic doctors were listened to with rapt attention, and so too were those of some practitioners whose certificates were less respectable. The information about the economy yielded by the most advanced electro-cardiographs and the portents perceived by the most esoteric diviners were alike ambiguous. And whatever the monetary state of health which the economy was showing and whatever the complexities of the malady with which it was afflicted, a sober diagnosis would have had to note a large element of hypochondria.

The events of the last week of May hardened the attitudes of business toward government wherever they had been soft before and gave new meaning to that splendid abstraction, "the business community." As put differently (by a columnist for the labor press), business was "in a darkly churlish mood," and the captains of industry were "about as disposed to cooperate with John F. Kennedy at the moment as they would be with Karl Marx." One story was even repeated to the President at a June press conference that business folk were saying, "now we have him where we want him." Mr. Kennedy did not believe the sentiment was real.

Inevitably, the attacks upon the President produced another

current of opinion. The remark reported to Mr. Kennedy became evidence for a theory of business conspiracy against government. The stock-market crash had been manipulated by some little group of willful men so ideologically-minded that they were willing to see stupendous losses to the value of the stock options with which large corporations had come to reward their leaders, and all for the purpose of destroying Mr. Kennedy. This theory came in time to cover all the events of steel, even to the extent of crediting Mr. Blough and his associates with a detailed foreknowledge of just what would happen if Mr. Kennedy took the steps that in fact he took.

It was a strange period. One of its most curious features was that understanding of what had in fact happened did not grow but instead diminished. The stories about the stock-market crash were excellent illustrations of this. On the one hand Mr. Kennedy's part in the steel crisis was blamed for causing the market decline, on the other hand big business was accused of manipulating the decline as punishment for Mr. Kennedy. Both sets of accusers ignored the fact that the market had been in a steep decline since the last week in March, well before the crisis in steel. Both sets ignored the high levels of prices in relation to earnings that had been prevailing before the decline began. Both ignored the price breaks which had already occurred in other markets of the world.

There was also a curious although somewhat more understandable confusion as to what had actually happened in the steel crisis itself. Again the confusion was shared by people of opposite viewpoints. On the one hand, the President was given credit for forceful action eminently worthy of a President and national leader, and on the other hand the President was condemned for the exercise of an extreme of power. The second group was responsible for the most remarkable examples of this confusion. The joint Senate-House Republican leadership issued a manifesto which carried this statement: ". . . The President directed or supported a series of governmental actions that imperiled basic American rights, went far beyond the law, and were more characteristic of a police state than a free government." The document then listed nine actions of the government to support the charge. A little later, the *New Republic* carried an article on "the President's short war against steel." This article by a well-known liberal lawyer listed a total of fourteen things that the administration had done in the course of "forcing the companies to their knees." Its conclusion was that the President did no service to freedom. A highly respected business-school dean produced a shorter list of actions, but said that this list, if true, might "represent the most serious threat to American civil liberties since the Civil War."

Apparently the compilers of these lists saw nothing ludicrous in the fact that the "actions" by the administration included items such as the following: "Treasury Department officials indicated they were at once reconsidering the planned increase in depreciation rates for steel"; "It was reported that the Administration was considering new, stringent antitrust legislation": "The White House held meetings of high officials to consider further government action." The various lists included other examples of excessive action by the government: the President's press conference, and the different investigations by the Federal Trade Commission, the special grand jury in New York, and committees in Congress. They made much of the behavior of the FBI and of the Defense Department's order to contractors to buy steel from firms which sold cheapest. There were also charges that Treasury agents opened investigations into the personal income-tax returns of steel executives. These charges have been convincingly denied.

The remarkable evaluation of these actions was probably a tribute to the Kennedy administration's skill in public relations. Nothing that was actually done was in any way illegal, or indeed particularly extraordinary. The investigations were according to law and were activities of which the steel industry had had much experience and against which it had defended itself very effectively over a period of more than half a century. Presidents had held press conferences before, and so also had steel executives. On occasion both sides had spoken with little restraint. And the award of contracts to those who would sell at lower prices than others would have seemed to be well within the code of capitalism.

Ultimately, the curious fact that which these lists should have demonstrated was that the administration had done very little indeed during the crisis. The length of the lists and the nature of the items should have suggested what was obvious, that there was almost no power to deal with the crisis at the President's disposal save persuasion and appeal to public opinion.

There was, however, a theory which perhaps came as a second thought when the character of these various presidential deeds had received examination. It was that the threat to freedom came not from any one of those deeds, but from their sheer number and from the co-ordination of government. By this theory, particular powers (assuming them to be that) were being exercised for purposes other than those for which they were created. It was a case of Massachusetts machine politics played upon a national scale. Just as a ward heeler might prevent the removal of garbage from the home of an opponent's supporter, so Mr. Kennedy had precipitated Congressional and other investigations of steel. This presumed that the investigations were irrelevant. The theory also implied that one of the defenses of American freedom was the lack of administrative co-ordination within the executive branch. Here it seemed to rely upon the fact that often the American government has been split by agencies beholden to particular interest groups and that conflicts have developed among these spokesmen agencies. The presentation of this frequently observed trait as a constitutional merit of the American system was a new contribution to political theory.

Behind the question of the propriety of the actions of the administration during the crisis there lay another; what effect did these actions have upon the course of events? There was a general belief, one certainly present in the views just examined, that Mr. Kennedy and his associates had undone the price increase. It is impossible to say categorically either that this was so or that it was not. Nevertheless, there is much to suggest that the acts of government may have had only a minor effect upon the decision of April 13. It is known now that there was serious doubt within U. S. Steel itself whether the price increase could be made to stand. These doubts were expressed by the representatives of the corporation's commercial department. Their doubts were shared quite independently, and before the increase was rescinded, by some competent and conservative academic economists. Moreover the editor of the magazine *Steel*, writing just after the increase had been withdrawn, commented: "We wish the increase could have been market-tested. We are not at all sure it would have lasted. The industry has been having trouble realizing quoted prices on some products for several years."

The positive evidence, however, lay in the events which actually preceded the withdrawal by U. S. Steel. The issue was in doubt until Inland Steel announced it would not increase its prices. The Inland action made Bethlehem, which shares in the Chicago market, very vulnerable. When Bethlehem withdrew, Big Steel was left without hope. Mr. Joseph Block, president of Inland, has been very emphatic on this matter. In his eyes there was no doubt whatsoever that his own firm's decision made the price increase by any firm untenable. He has suggested that action by Kaiser, or even a smaller firm, in refusing to raise prices would have had the same impact. The action of U. S. Steel in following the price decreases of Kaiser on the Pacific coast during October 1962, tends to confirm the judgment of Mr. Block.

This, however, may only reduce the question to the problem of what determined the Inland decision. Mr. Block has said that a view of the national interest prevailed with him. It was an interesting vision, as he described it. The nearness of the labor settlement in time, the continuing negotiations between the union and the smaller companies, and the great weakness of the market were the elements of the national interest as he saw it. The last of these was by far the most important. He agreed that the governmental intervention had played some part, but how great he was not willing to say. It is difficult not to believe that the overwhelming consideration at Inland was the weakness of demand in the market.

There is a danger in accepting such an evaluation, in that an element of bias is involved. Probably, steel executives would prefer to believe that their actions had been determined by strictly business considerations rather than by words or acts of government. This is a bias which is shared by labor leaders, who have also minimized the influence of government on their own actions, particularly in the decision to reach an early accord in steel. This bias in industry arises insensibly from the ideological commitment to the belief that nothing that government can do can have any effect upon the workinug of economic forces. The bias in labor arises from the fact that if the union membership were to become convinced that governmental action in economic matters could be effective, it might prefer to give its loyalty to government rather than to the union. With the steel industry there was also an incentive to protect itself against a possible charge that the industry had been acting politically; a demonstration that only economic motives had been at work would be defense against this unsettling accusation. However, the 1962 affair of steel, with its emotional aftermath, did give support to that curious but by no means uncommon doctrine that government action can have no effect in economic affairs and that the effects of government action are always evil.

Nevertheless, the evidence seems strong that considerations of the market largely determined the ending of the steel crisis. This, perhaps, was the one really revolutionary aspect of the entire affair. Until this week in April, the outstanding characteristic of the American steel industry in the twentieth century had been price leadership by U. S. Steel. On the other hand, it is quite probable that the actions of Mr. Kennedy and Arthur J. Goldberg, the Secretary of Labor, had an appreciable influence upon the decision of the union to make an early and a modest settlement.

The unraveling of these decisions, with its implicit suppositions of motives, is both dangerous and artificial. The motives are ultimately unknowable, probably even to the principals. Nevertheless, there were in the situations of 1962 a few factors of rationality, rationality within different contexts perhaps, but yet rationality. The United States government and U. S. Steel are both large organizations. The character of these organizations and the situations within which they were compelled to operate did create impulsions which would have been felt in some degree by whatever individuals found themselves in positions of direction.

In this setting, then, why did U. S. Steel make the increase, and at the time and in the manner that it did? Why did the Kennedy administration respond so violently to the price increase?

The second of these questions is fairly easy to answer. The new administration was committed to an actionist philosophy. Nevertheless, economically it was caught in a trap of impotence: unless the scale of the balance-of-payments problem could be reduced, there could be no realization of the promises of growth and full employment. In administration eyes, the pressure of wage costs was a central force in this problem and in the closely related matter of inflation. Moreover, in Secretary Goldberg, Mr. Kennedy had a lieutenant who gladly sought to affect the pattern of industrial relations and who committed the administration to a policy of intervention in labor disputes which developed its own momentum. For each of these areas of policy, steel was the ultimate test. As events developed, the policy makers of the administration came to believe that an understanding had been achieved, however much it may have later astonished Mr. Blough. When the labor settlement arrived and was then followed by a price increase, all of the economic objectives of the administration were threatened. Much more important than this, however, the character and the power of the presidency were at stake. The President had to respond.

The decision of United States Steel to raise prices is in many ways more mysterious. The decision, however, did have intense political effects. With these in full view shortly after the crisis, *Fortune* noted a theory that Mr. Blough was acting as a "business statesman." Thus, "Kennedy's letter of last September 6 poised over the industry a threat of 'jawbone control' of prices. For the sake of his company, the industry, and the nation, Blough sought a way to break through the bland 'harmony' that has recently prevailed between government and business." By this theory, the action by U. S. Steel could be seen as precisely designed to alienate the President from labor and to curtail the President's power to act with effectiveness in economic affairs. It is an interesting theory, for it would suggest that the incomprehension of U. S. Steel's intention by the administration was understood by the executives of Big Steel. It also implies that the political position in which the President was placed was foreseen.

Both of these theories unfortunately rest upon suppositions of motives within U. S. Steel. In so emotion-laden a situation as that of 1962, motives are effectively unknowable, especially in retrospect. Only the acts and the results are visible, and those only partially. Nevertheless, it is evident that the decision to increase prices was a mistake; the increase had to be rescinded. However the matter was seen before the increase, this was a decision with both economic and political components.

Regarded in narrow terms and in retrospect, there are good grounds for believing that the price increase might have been successful politically. There was a long record of struggle between U. S. Steel and the government. This was with only small exceptions—those on basing-point pricing and the wage increase of 1956—a record of U. S. Steel success. Second, there was a clear absence of any strong presidential power to cope with such an issue other than by persuasion. The temper of the nation offered the corporation excellent opportunity to compete in this area of power. Third, the incident of the Business Advisory Council suggested that Mr. Kennedy would yield when pressed. Even after the event of April 13, some Washington observers suggested that if the price increase had not been across the board, the President would have acquiesced. Certainly, with selective increases perhaps moderated by a few unimportant decreases, the position of the presidency would not have been threatened as it was by the general increase. Fourth, there are the indications that the actions of government may have had only a slight part in bringing about withdrawal of the increase. Oddly enough, then, it may be true that in a narrow sense the Corporation's decision was politically sound but commercially mistaken.

In a large sense, the crisis of April 1962, was a conflict between two centers of power, the corporation and the President. And in this sense it was primarily a political struggle. At no time in its history had the corporation ever been a simple economic unit. It was Judge Elbert H. Gary's (first chairman of the board) peculiar mark of genius to have recognized this and to have seen his task in these terms. During his later years he suggested the essential character of U. S. Steel when he said that U. S. Steel is "a semi-public enterprise." The same conception was illustrated by the complaint of a later corporation chairman, Myron L. Taylor, that he had trouble in finding "men who will leave private business and devote themselves to the corporation." And the idea was, perhaps unconsciously, put forward by Mr. Blough and his associates in the very simple explanation of the 1962 price increase, that U. S. Steel "needed" the higher prices. Such a statement could not have been made by the proprietor of a corner variety store: the market would support higher prices for him or it would not. If the prices which he could obtain within the competitive system would permit him to meet his costs, he would succeed; if they did not, he would fail. The regular incidence of many thousand business failures each year is one of the concomitants of the modern economy.

Yet to say this in conjunction with the difficulties of U. S. Steel, once the greatest of corporations, verges on the outrageous. This is an entirely different order of organization, one whose very being has rested upon a long-term tenure of power. It has been power of a particular kind, indeed, power in the market. Nevertheless, this power has inevitably come into repeated conflict with the power of government, increasingly in later years with the power of the presidency.

As it always must with power, a problem of legitimacy existed from the very first days of the U. S. Steel Corporation. If the actions of the corporation were in any substantial measure free from the restraints of a competitive market, those actions were open to question and challenge. Why these actions and not others? Why these and not lower prices? There was no absolute basis upon which any decision or any action could be justified. If the assumption that the impersonal force of the market determined the course of economic events was breached, then there were no unassailable criteria and an abyss had opened.

U. S. Steel has been sensitive to the problem throughout its existence. Judge Gary followed a policy of restraint in the exercise of Big Steel power and persuasively argued that this power had not been abused. Nevertheless, this was a vulnerable policy, for there was no objective basis for asserting that the Corporation's actions were correct. Others could differ with his judgment and many did. The later policy of the Corporation was to deny the existence of power in its hands. This also was a vulnerable policy, for the firm's great size seemed to imply the reality of such power. Nevertheless, the alternatives to these policies, dissolution of U. S. Steel into several separate units, or control of its actions by government, were not acceptable to the Corporation.

The problem of legitimacy—of criteria—has always been at the heart of government also. Just as nobody in U. S. Steel could offer an indisputable justification for the prices that were asked for steel, nobody in government could say indisputably what those prices should be or why. However, the problem of making choices and decisions where objective criteria are lacking is very common in government, and as a consequence much attention has been given to the means for coping with it. Whenever possible, answers to questions where this condition exists are sought in established laws and precedents. When these are unavailable, the task of choosing devolves upon Congress, the President, and other elected representatives of the people. The existence of so many choices is a major reason why so much thought and care is given to the mechanics of representation and consultation with the public.

As he looked back upon the events of 1962, Mr. Blough asked, "What is the public interest? And who, if anyone, is the rightful custodian of the public interest?" He answered his first question, saying that "the public interest is the incredibly diverse lawful interests of each of the more than 185 million human beings who live in this Republic." The implicit answer to his second question is that everyone is the custodian of the public interest, a conclusion which it would be difficult to dispute.

Nevertheless, the problem remains. Some of the diverse lawful interests of Americans include concerns which great numbers of them share, concerns such as economic growth, full employment, and a favorable solution to the balance-of-payments problem. How should these be weighed against other legitimate interests and who should do the weighing?

Mr. Blough has said that people in management must consider their employers (the stockholders), their employees, and their customers, all of whom are part of the public. In this sense, a concern by U. S. Steel for the larger elements of the public interest is praiseworthy and necessary. Given the existence of choices among differing interests, choices in which standards for decision are lacking, however, the corporation is at a disadvantage in any disagreement with government. The mechanics of representation by which the corporation is linked to the different members of its constituency as defined by Mr. Blough are much more nebulous than the mechanics by which the government of the United States is linked to its constituency. Moreover, the constituency of the government of the United States is much more explicitly inclusive than that of U. S. Steel.

Ultimately, the constituency of the presidency is the only unambiguously comprehensive constituency in the nation. Whatever the degree of wisdom that the President brings to his task, the task requires that he take into account all the diverse elements of the public interest. Moreover, he is accountable to all the people of the United States for his actions and his decisions. The means of enforcing accountability may be less than perfect, but the awesome fact remains that the presidency is the only office in America with a constituency of the entire nation. Moreover, the capacity to co-ordinate different components of policy in a world of in-

creasing complexity and persistent danger is inescapably concentrated in the presidency.

The responsibility which derives from this is enormous. It is
unmatched in any other office in the world. Nevertheless, the
power which accompanies this responsibility is ill-defined and
often uncertain. Article II of the Constitution, which deals with
the President's power, is one of the vaguest parts of the document.
This lack of precision permits the expansion of power in the
hands of the President during time of national crisis. With sufficient public support in such a time, a President may do things
under the Constitution that would in normal times be forbidden
him. In another sense, however, the vagueness in the grant of
power to the President is very restrictive. The constitutional pre-
sumption throughout American government is that power not
explicitly granted is forbidden. In times other than those of crisis,
the limitations upon presidential action are narrow.

There is a problem of great and probably increasing seriousness in this condition. It is that in situations which lie between national extremity and normality, situations that may be
expected with some frequency at least as long as the Cold War
lasts, presidential responsibility may be severely out of proportion
to presidential power. In placid times it is sufficient that presidential power should be narrow, for the checking of one private
ambition by another will produce results that at least by the
standards of the past are adequate. In time of overt crisis, when
the reality is plain and obvious, Congress can be expected to give
authority for action if action then is possible. However, there
may be occasions in the twilight between normality and crisis in
which a President is forced to betray a lack of power commensurate with the need for action. While the immediate consequences
of this betrayal may be serious in themselves, the train of events
that may be released by such an exposure could be disastrous.
Power is not solely a grant of authority under a constitutional
provision. It is also a capacity for action which rests upon intan-
gibles of previous history, public confidence, and prestige. These
elements of power are fundamental to the modern presidency. If
they are weak, the presidency is diminished and the republic is
endangered.

The affair of steel in 1962 poses this problem. The hasty judgment of some who were themselves involved in that affair and of

others who only noted the tenor of the language of the presidential response was that the President wielded a gross excess of power. This judgment was correct only in that it touched on the central issue, power. Otherwise it was mistaken. The President did oppose the price increase announced by United States Steel, and the price increase was rescinded. The sequence, however, did not represent cause and effect. For this one time at least, the frequent contention of steel-industry leaders that strong competitive market forces were at work in the industry was correct. These forces were much more important in bringing about abandonment of the price increase than the actions of the President. Those actions showed weakness, not power.

On the large issue, the affair was ominous. Whatever the intentions of Mr. Blough and his associates in U. S. Steel, the announcement of the price increase amounted to a direct challenge of the presidency. If the action by Big Steel had been successful, the power of the presidency could only have been diminished. The ultimate results of such success are unfathomable, but it is not unthinkable that they would have been felt in Europe and in the Caribbean. If U. S. Steel should not have placed the President in such a situation, perhaps the President should not have made himself open to such a challenge. The danger implicit in such a bargain as was attempted, an exchange of support in achieving a labor settlement in return for price stability, was that its terms would not be kept and that the government would be left without recourse. In the event, the danger became reality. President Kennedy gave a virtuoso performance of simulating action and the situation was successfully disguised. Perhaps his greatest achievement lay in holding the diverse elements of his administration together and creating a façade of unity in government. This required intense effort and much skill, but it could not have continued for long. Events rescued the President. Nevertheless, the administration's venture came perilously close to an exposure of impotence.

There was irony in the outcome of the affair of 1962. As the commuters nursed their sense of injury and rode along to Scarsdale, the overwhelming impression was that the power that had prevailed was the power of the presidency. The real power that had been displayed, however, was this time the one that they approved, the power of the market.

The Budget and Economic Growth

THE RESEARCH AND POLICY COMMITTEE
OF THE COMMITTEE FOR
ECONOMIC DEVELOPMENT

The Committee for Economic Development is a group of 200 businessmen educators interested in promoting economic growth, stability, and opportunity. It sponsors research upon which it bases findings and recommendations. The following statement was issued in 1959.

PROMOTING ECONOMIC STABILITY AND GROWTH

THERE IS a natural temptation in the political process to yield one at a time to the demands of particular groups for increasing the particular expenditures in which they are interested. This, rather than any general philosophy favoring deficits and bigger budgets, is the main obstacle to the achievement of the policy we recommend. However, in the current debate a number of arguments have been advanced which seem to attach the label of "economic growth" to every proposal for more expenditures, regardless of their character and whether or not financed by more taxes. Since these arguments tend to confuse and weaken the general discipline that is necessary as a counterpoise to particular interests in budget expansion, it is important to analyze them carefully.

The arguments about the connection between bigger budgets and growth have popular appeal not only because they promise an escape from difficult choices but also because there is a certain *element* of truth in them.

1. It is true, in general, that when unemployment is high a Federal deficit of a certain size and duration will contribute to the rapid restoration of high employment, and will do so without serious risk of inflation. That is why this Committee has always recommended a budget policy that would generate deficits in recessions.

2. It is true that the increase of some kinds of Federal expenditures at certain rates would contribute to the growth of the output

that the economy produces when it works at high employment. This is particularly true of expenditures that increase the nation's stock of productive assets, that add to knowledge, and that improve the competence of the working force.

3. It is also true that the growth of the economy requires the increase at an appropriate rate of certain expenditures to service the growing population and economic activity.

4. It is also true that the growth of the economy permits us to increase certain government expenditures from which the population enjoys benefits just as it permits us to increase private expenditures.

These propositions would be strong arguments against a policy of balancing the budget every year, whatever the circumstances, and against a policy of holding expenditures constant. But they are not arguments against a budget policy which, having generated a budget deficit of $13 billion in response to the recession of 1958, now proposes to bring the budget into balance when high employment is regained. And they do not imply that the proper response to a budget proposing cash expenditures 32 per cent higher than those of five years earlier is "More!"

The important questions about the relation between the budget and growth are not whether deficits in general or expenditures in general are good for growth. The important questions are, first, when are deficits constructive for achieving high employment and when are they harmful; and, second, what types of Federal expenditures, and of what amounts, are good for growth?

BUDGET POLICY AND HIGH EMPLOYMENT

The basic reason for running a Federal deficit during periods of recession is that it helps to sustain private demand and to promote recovery. By the same reasoning, when private demand is high and rising and threatens to exceed the nation's economic capacity to produce, the government should collect more in taxes than it spends—in other words, realize surpluses—in order to restrain demand. (As we indicate later, these surpluses would also provide capital for growth.) Deficits in prosperous times, particularly when they are financed through the expansion of bank credit, inevitably aggravate the inflationary pressures associated with economic expansion.

While these general principles are fairly well understood and can readily be applied when the situation is clearly one of recession or high employment, controversy arises when they are to be applied during periods of transition from recession to high employment. Part of the problem of planning under present circumstances is that the economy is in just such a transition period now. And we are faced with the necessity of making decisions about the budget for the fiscal year 1959–60, which runs until June 30, 1960. It is important to note that the decision applies to a year which ends 15 months from now, when conditions are likely to be very different from what they are today.

In the current fiscal year, which ends on June 30, 1959, it is estimated that there will be a Federal cash deficit of about $13 billion—the highest deficit ever, except in World War II. Almost all of this deficit will be the result of the recession. Receipts will be about $9 billion lower than they would have been if high employment had been steadily maintained. Unemployment compensation payments and certain other expenditures were increased by the recession. Expenditures for highways, housing and some other purposes were deliberately increased to stimulate business activity. The large cash deficit, most of which developed automatically, helped to stop the decline in the spring of 1953 and undoubtedly contributed to the subsequent recovery.

The current rate of deficit (March 1959) is much smaller than the $13 billion estimated for the whole fiscal year 1958–59. This is the result of the recovery in production, incomes and employment since mid-1958. Gross national product is probably running about 6 per cent above the average for 1958. It is difficult to assign a precise and significant figure to the current rate of deficit, because of uncertain seasonal factors and the lag of tax collections behind accruals. But with present income levels, existing expenditure programs and tax rates would probably yield a deficit of less than $5 billion. The question is not whether we should have a balanced budget *now*, in March 1959, when 6 per cent of the labor force is unemployed. That would obviously be unwise.

We have before us a proposed budget that would be balanced *if a certain assumed rate of recovery is achieved.* The underlined words are important. The 1959–60 budget will *not* be balanced if economic activity remains at its present level. In fact, if economic activity remains at its present level, the deficit will also remain approximately at its present level—because almost all of the shift from a $13 billion deficit in 1958–59 to a balanced budget in 1959–60 results from the rise in economic activity which has already occurred and which is assumed to continue. Thus the budget proposed for fiscal 1960 is essentially "neutral," in the sense that its stimulating effect upon the economy would remain constant if economic activity remained constant and would gradually diminish as economic activity revived. The fiscal 1960 budget would be in balance if gross national product in calendar 1959 reached the $473 billion level assumed in the budget, or about 8 per cent above 1958. Since we started the year at a lower level this implies a figure of almost $490 billion at the end of the year, which would be very close to a high employment level of activity.[1]

We believe that the proposed budget is a reasonable adaptation to the prospects and uncertainties of the year ahead. It would not impose a strong repressive influence upon a recovery that is not yet complete or fully assured. But the budget would not add a further stimulus, in the form of an enlarged deficit, to a recovery which has already made substantial progress. We believe that the most realistic expectation for any further period about which there is no clear evidence to the contrary is that private demands for goods and services will be strong enough to produce high employment while the Federal budget is in balance. There is no clear ground for believing that 1959–60 will be an exception to this general rule. Moreover, we now stand fairly close to—although not at—high employment. In these circumstances it is a good general principle to set tax rates and expenditures so that they would yield at least a balance in the cash budget at high employment. To do otherwise, and budget for a deficit at high employment, would add little if anything—even in the short run —to economic growth, but would greatly intensify the danger of further inflation.

There is a possibility that reemployment will lag and unsatisfactorily high unemployment persist during 1959–60. This possibility, which is within the range of the usual uncertainties surrounding any period a year ahead, does not justify departure from the general rule of balancing the cash budget at high em-

1. We define high employment to be employment of 96 per cent of the labor force, after adjustment for seasonal variation.

ployment. But it does call for flexibility in adapting the available instruments of policy to the emerging situation. This applies particularly to monetary policy. Moreover, as already noted, if recovery lags the deficit will not be eliminated.

To reduce both the likelihood and the hardship of unemployment, action should be taken this year to improve the nation's unemployment compensation system. In many states, the level of benefits is still inadequate in relation to wages, and the duration of the benefits during periods of prolonged unemployment is too short. As of the beginning of 1959, roughly a third of the workers covered by state unemployment insurance systems were in states where the maximum weekly benefit is less than 40 per cent of their average weekly wages. And one-fifth of the workers were in states paying benefits for a maximum of less than 26 weeks. We believe the states should raise the maximum weekly benefits, where necessary, to at least half of the workers' regular earnings and to lengthen the maximum term of benefits to 26 weeks. In addition, in many states firms with one to three persons are still not covered, and Congress should extend coverage to them. These changes would not only alleviate the hardships of prolonged unemployment; they would also improve the automatic stabilizing effect of the Federal budget.

With a Federal budget that automatically generates large deficits during recessions, it is preferable to plan to balance the budget at high employment, and to count on easing monetary policy if necessary to stimulate the economy, than to plan on a budget deficit and count on monetary restriction to curb any inflationary tendencies that may result. It is exceedingly difficult to apply adequate monetary restrictions in the face of booming private demand for credit if the Federal Treasury is at the same time both refunding large maturities of debt and borrowing new money to finance a deficit.

We believe that it should be the basic policy of the Federal government not only to balance the cash budget but also to run a substantial cash surplus at high employment. This would greatly assist in the task of conducting anti-inflationary monetary and debt management policies. Equally important, a cash surplus would make saving available for financing private investment that would promote growth. When the government retires debt, the funds received by bondholders in exchange for their bonds are used for other investments. And, under conditions of high employment, they are likely to be invested directly, or indirectly through the purchase of securities, in enterprises seeking funds for expansion. This important link between surpluses at high employment and growth has been overlooked by many people in recent discussions of budgetary policy.

Interest on the Federal debt has increased rapidly in recent years and will account for almost 7 per cent of total cash expenditures in fiscal 1960. To avoid a further increase in this drain on the budget, and if possible to reduce it, is another reason for generating surpluses at high employment.

We do not recommend that an effort be made to achieve a substantial surplus in 1959–60, under the economic conditions assumed in the budget, for two reasons. Even if high employment is regained during 1959–60, the budget results for that year will still be affected by the lower level of economic activity early in calendar 1959. Moreover, expenditure commitments for next year in existing programs, appropriations and obligations are already so large as to make any significant net reduction in the budget almost impossible. But every effort should be made now to avoid expenditure commitments that will be obstacles to the achievement of a surplus in the future.

We do not want to suggest that a cash surplus during periods of growth is a sure guarantee of price stability. Prices rose in 1956 and 1957 when there were surpluses averaging $3 billion. It would be foolhardy to predict that prices will be stable if surpluses of these magnitudes are planned for the time when the current recovery restores high employment. Many other factors, including the behavior of business and labor and the firmness of the monetary authorities in preventing inflationary increases in the supply of money and credit, will have a bearing on the final outcome. But we do know that, if fiscal and monetary policies are lax when demand is strong, it will be impossible to keep prices from rising. A decision to run a deficit at high employment would be a long step toward validating the expectation of continuing inflation which the 1956–57 experience generated.

FEDERAL EXPENDITURES AND ECONOMIC GROWTH

Promoting economic growth is more than a matter of regaining and maintaining high employment. It is also, and over any extended period of time much more importantly, a matter of increasing the nation's *capacity* to produce a larger volume of goods and services. This has been done in the past and is being done now by increasing the skills of workers, increasing the amount and variety of capital, and promoting innovation and technological improvement.

As we have already stated, a balanced budget and a surplus in periods of high employment are *means* to enable the economy to grow without inflation. Deficit financing in prosperous times will contribute to inflation, but it will not increase the rate of sustainable growth—simply because deficits do not in themselves create the conditions necessary to accelerate growth. In fact, continued inflation may distort the normal incentives for efficiency in business and increased productivity of labor and thus endanger growth itself.

Although our knowledge about the forces that promote growth is at a rudimentary stage, we do know that many of the activities performed by the Federal government have very little to do with growth. In fact, some of its programs and policies are designed to prevent adjustments in the economy that would contribute to a more effective allocation of the nation's resources. By artificially supporting farm prices, for example, the Federal government encourages too many farmers to remain in farming who could earn a better livelihood elsewhere. The stockpiling programs sustain output of metals and minerals which are not needed either for defense purposes or for production in the private economy. Tariffs and import quotas prevent us from purchasing goods at lower prices from foreign producers. And there are numerous proposals to keep labor and capital in areas and industries where they are no longer needed.

We do not pretend to know precisely what expenditures of the Federal government, and in what amounts, will produce a given increase in the nation's growth rate. This is a matter deserving careful study and analysis. But a number of things can be said to clarify some of the considerations involved in making this judgment.

1. Some kinds of Federal expenditures should increase because the nation's population and economy are growing. In part, this is a matter of increasing facilities, simply because more people are using them, so that productivity will not fall. In part, these increasing expenditures represent more public consumption out of

our increasing national product, and the proper amount depends on the taxpayers' choice between public consumption and private consumption.

2. Many service and housekeeping activities performed by Federal agencies, e.g., regulation of security markets, the postal services, and collection and dissemination of statistical information, are essential to the orderly functioning of the economy. The harm that would be done to the economy by a sharp curtailment of many of these services would be out of proportion to their costs. But the aggregate of such expenditures is only a small fraction of the Federal budget; and, in any event, they are for the most part not involved in the current debate over the worthwhileness of additional Federal expenditures.

3. Some kinds of Federal government expenditures *contribute* to growth through the investment process, either in human or physical capital. And, like private investment, Federal investments should be worth more than their costs. In determining costs, it is essential to include not only the cost of the resources that would be otherwise be used for other purposes either in the private economy or by state and local governments, but also the indirect cost of any reduction in work, saving, and investment incentives induced by the taxes required to pay for the expenditure.

To illustrate, the Federal government contributes to growth by encouraging *research* to develop new knowledge in science and technology and to promote the nation's health. An airways *modernization* program helps to provide greater safety and efficiency in air transportation. A *highway improvement* program is also essential to facilitate commerce and trade. Expenditures on *education,* for which the Federal government is already spending close to $500 million per year, may contribute to growth. As the following table shows, the Federal government's expenditures on these programs will amount to about $10 billion in fiscal year 1960, nearly 3 times as much as the corresponding expenditures five years earlier and 5 times as much as the amounts spent ten years earlier.

Even with respect to the kinds of public investment that are clearly productive there is always a question of *how much* is worth while. Highways are productive, but this does not mean that $3 billion of investment in highways is necessarily better than

$2 billion and that $4 billion is better still, any more than it would necessarily be good to double investment in any particular private industry. The problem is to find the amount of investment for any purpose that is not only productive but more productive than the best alternatives.

TABLE 1.

| Program | Fiscal Years (millions of dollars) | | |
	1950 (actual)	1955 (actual)	1960 (proposed)
Research and Development, total			
Major national security	871	1,804	4,572
Other	209	281	912
Highways	498	647	3,046[2]
Aviation and space[1]	157	177	576
Education[1]	73	324	474
Health[1]	204	202	237
Total	2,012	3,435	9,817

1. Excluding research and development. Amounts for health and education also exclude expenditures by the Veterans Administration and by the Department of Defense for these activities.

2. Practically all of this amount is accounted for by the expenditures of the Federal Highway Trust Fund, which are financed by excises on highway users.

Source: Bureau of the Budget.

As we have already noted, the budget for 1960 not only proposes expenditures for government functions of kinds that clearly promote growth. It proposes much larger expenditures for these functions than have been made in the past. Perhaps some of these expenditures should be even larger. But it is surely erroneous and misleading to criticize the budget as if it proposed no expenditures, or reduced expenditures, or small expenditures for growth.

4. Even if a particular governmental activity is necessary for growth, it is not obvious that this activity should necessarily be performed or financed by the Federal government. Most of the governmental services required in our dynamic, growing economy are actually provided by the states and local governments. Education, waste disposal, construction and operation of water facilities, police and fire protection and other direct governmental services have historically been state-local functions, because the

needs for these services vary greatly throughout the country and can best be judged by officials who are most familiar with these needs. It is true that the states and local governments are now encountering financial difficulties in providing such services. But to some extent at least, these difficulties are traceable to the fact that the taxes levied by the Federal government are extremely high.

In brief, more growth is not guaranteed by a higher level of expenditures, either in the private or the public sector. The crucial test is whether the expenditures are directed into productive investments in human and physical capital. The American people rightfully expect their government to invest in activities that will promote growth. But they should be willing to pay for them and also to do without those things that are either wasteful or unnecessary. However, as we shall indicate later, a large share of the current outlays of the Federal government does not contribute to growth and there is little evidence that most new proposals for Federal spending would significantly improve this unsatisfactory record.

Revenue and the Redistribution of Wealth

JOHN MORTON BLUM

John Morton Blum is Professor of History at Yale University. This article is from his book, From the Morgenthau Diaries: Years of Crisis, 1928–1938, *published in 1959.*

THE PROBLEMS of depression, the cost of relief, and the inequities in American society gave taxation special importance as an instrument of public policy during the 1930's. Tax schedules affected more than the government's income. They had significance, too, for national recovery and for social reform. "The primary interest of the Treasury . . . relates to . . . revenue," Henry Morgenthau said early in his term. As long as he was Secretary of the Treasury, that interest was to predominate. As he also observed, however, "taxation in any form has many collateral effects . . . and . . . there is a national duty to avoid tax laws which produce undesirable social consequences and a like duty to correct evils produced by existing tax legislation."

Every tax program had to compromise among its several aims, and as changing conditions warranted a changing emphasis, Morganthau concentrated now upon one, now upon another aspect of the tax problem. During his first months in office, while other issues absorbed him, he nevertheless set forth the principles that guided his policies. The New Deal, he told the House Ways and Means Committee late in 1933, had an overwhelming mandate to improve the position of the underdog. Wealthy individuals were in far the best position to bear additional burdens, and increases in their income and estate taxes would have the desirable effect of reducing huge disparities in economic power. Before the Senate Judiciary Committee in 1934, he recommended closing the loopholes through which rich men and corporations avoided taxes, he emphasized the need for a constitutional amendment permitting taxation of the income from federal and local securities, which were tax exempt, and he appealed for additional funds for enforcement. He could say nothing more specific, for he was under instructions from President Roosevelt to leave the choice of new taxes to the Congress, and to comment only on the estimates of receipts from alternative schedules. The Revenue Act of 1934 raised slightly income, estate and gift taxes in the higher brackets, but it was at best only a beginning.

Indeed the Treasury had yet fully to develop its own policies, for the Republican Administrations of the 1920's had not recruited a staff of experts with the qualifications Morgenthau considered necessary for studying tax questions. As rapidly as he could, he put together a group of men, some permanent employees, some temporary consultants who undertook a comprehensive survey of the federal tax structure. This group included Herman Oliphant, Jacob Viner, and George Haas, who were already hard at work on many problems. Roswell Magill, a professor of tax law at Columbia University, later Under Secretary of the Treasury, gave general direction to the research. The three specialists who worked most closely and productively with Magill were Carl S. Shoup, also of Columbia, Roy Blough, a professor of economics formerly assistant director of research for Harry Hopkins, and Lawrence H. Seltzer, who in 1934 became George Haas's assistant director and chief economist. Guy Helvering, the head of the Internal Revenue Bureau, contributed useful information about tax enforcement.

By the end of the summer of 1934 Magill and his associates, who were cooperating with Congress in studying the British tax system, had reassessed the Treasury's purposes. Their reports provided Morgenthau with a series of recommendations designed to increase revenues and to dissolve dangerous concentrations of wealth. Armed with the information he needed, he was ready to try to enlist the President's support.

On December 11, 1934, Morgenthau took his proposals to the White House. The first called for a graduated inheritance tax to supplement the existing estate tax.[1] Such a tax would bring the proportion of revenue the United States collected from estates closer to that collected by the British government. Because inheritance taxes could be in large part avoided through gifts made before death, the Treasury further suggested either raising gift taxes or taxing gifts as ordinary income.

These recommendations clearly envisaged some redistribution of national wealth, a prospect that men of means naturally found

1. [An estate tax falls upon the total estate a man bequeaths; an inheritance tax, upon the individual shares of his heirs. *Editor*]

radical. Their attitude in no way deterred Morgenthau for, as he saw it, gross economic inequities were dangerous not only in themselves but also because they seemed to justify the demands of men like Huey Long for frankly confiscatory programs. Long promised to make every man a king on $2500 a year. The aged Dr. Francis E. Townsend won thousands of followers, especially in the Far West, by proposing $200 a month for all over sixty years old. Compared to such panaceas, the Treasury's recommendations were mild. Furthermore, Morgenthau had excellent precedents. Theodore Roosevelt had supported an inheritance tax as early as 1907 and during 1934 several congressional committees had given the idea serious consideration.

The second item in the Treasury's program was an intercorporate dividend tax designed to break up holding companies. Herman Oliphant and Felix Frankfurter in particular had pressed this scheme upon the Secretary as a means of preventing a recurrence of the skullduggery which had so marked the 1920's. Adventurers owning only a minority of a corporation's stock had been able through holding company devices to control a corporation, waste its assets and manipulate its securities for their own gain. Morgenthau saw in taxation the leverage to make holding companies reorder their affairs. As things stood, only the corporation first earning income paid a tax on it. The Treasury now proposed that each corporation receiving dividends from that income should also pay taxes. This would make holding companies with several tiers of subsidiaries unduly expensive. The Treasury also recommended revising the corporate income tax so as to make business mergers unattractive. For the long run, Morgenthau suggested scaling the tax on corporations according to their size.

A third major item in the Secretary's report to Roosevelt was a tax on undistributed corporate earnings. He asked, too, for the taxation of future issues of federal and local bonds, and for a reduction in tax exemptions for mineral depletions.

While Roosevelt, who initially considered the Treasury's recommendations premature, kept the report on his desk, the Department had to reach a decision about social security taxes. In order to minimize deficit expenditures, Morgenthau advocated taxing employees as well as employers for the social insurance program. In a supporting memorandum of January 1935, George Haas noted that payroll taxes for unemployment and old-age insurance would divert funds from current consumption to saving, but he suggested postponing serious consideration of a less deflationary tax to a later date. Testifying before the House Ways and Means Committee, Morgenthau in February emphasized the need for a sound financial basis for social security, the desirability of avoiding heavy taxes on future generations, and therefore the importance of a sufficient scale of contributory taxes to cover pending benefit payments. He had earlier urged limiting the Department of Labor's original proposal for social security coverage in order to keep initial expenditures at a manageable level. He was in all respects a friend of old age and unemployment insurance, but while he supported the reforms, he tried to keep a firm hand on the budget. These were also the views of the Congress which wrote the legislation as the Treasury had hoped it would.

Yet Haas's memoranda raised a troublesome question. As he suggested, the contributory social security taxes would reduce the spending power of a multitude of consumers. The program Morgenthau had taken to Roosevelt would also cut potential private spending and private investment by its heavy levies on individual inheritances and corporate income. This prospect bothered Marriner Eccles, among others, and accounted for Oliphant's preference for paying the bonus by deficit financing rather than new taxes. Morgenthau completely disagreed with that reasoning. The social security legislation in no way abated his zeal for increasing federal revenues as well as for attacking corporate size and reducing inherited wealth. Late in May 1935 he resumed his efforts to have the President adopt the Treasury's proposals.

In spite of his disavowal of new taxation in his 1935 budget message, Roosevelt was coming gradually to Morgenthau's position. Troubled by the political challenge of Long and Townsend, he might well have hoped that intelligent liberalism in tax policy would damp the appeal of unintelligent radicalism. The President was, moreover, increasingly impatient with the "economic royalists," the men of large means who were criticizing the New Deal more and more sharply. In this situation, Morgenthau argued that, whether Congress acted on taxes or not, it was imperative for Roosevelt to state clearly where he stood on the subject.

During the first half of June the President gave continual

thought to drafts of a tax message which Morgenthau and his staff
and Raymond Moley and Felix Frankfurter prepared. Although
Moley was expected to put the finishing touches on the document,
he seriously objected to the Treasury's entire program, as to the
whole recent drift of the New Deal. Frankfurter, as Morgenthau
saw it, served largely as a sounding board for the Treasury's ideas.

As the work progressed, Roosevelt singled out as essential four
of the recommended taxes: the tax on corporations, graduated to
check the growth of monopoly; the intercorporate dividend tax;
higher surtaxes on individual incomes; and the inheritance tax.
He gave only incidental attention to the Treasury's other proposals. On several occasions Morgenthau urged him to say that he
would use the proceeds from an inheritance tax to balance the
budget, but the President resisted any reference to budget
balancing.

The message Roosevelt sent to Congress on June 19, 1935, was
part of a developing Administration attack on economic bigness,
which the President now looked upon as a remediable evil,
whereas in 1933 he had tended to consider it inevitable. The
Treasury's arguments had contributed to the change of mind that
his message revealed. Wealth in the modern world, Roosevelt
said, resulted from a combination of individual efforts. In spite
of the "great importance in our national life of the . . . ingenuity
of unusual individuals, the people in the mass have inevitably
helped to make large fortunes possible." The transmission of these
fortunes from generation to generation, he argued, was not consistent with American ideals. Accumulations of wealth, moreover,
perpetrated "great and undesirable concentration of control in a
relatively few individuals over the employment and welfare of
many, many others." He therefore recommended an inheritance
tax, and in order to make "vast concentrations of capital . . . carry
burdens commensurate with their . . . advantages," he also proposed a graduated tax on corporate income.

This unequivocal endorsement of tax reform pleased liberals in
both parties. Along with the New Dealers on the Hill, progres-
sives like Senators Borah, Norris, and La Follette supported the
President, as did William Green, the head of the American Federation of Labor. The Topeka *Daily Capitol* and Philadelphia
Record applauded the message, but most newspapers, including
the New York *Herald Tribune*, the *New York Times*, and the

Milwaukee *Journal* were antagonistic. The Boston *Transcript* called the President's proposals a "socialist experiment," and Raymond Moley later wrote that he felt Roosevelt was feuding with the rich. Speaking for most Republicans, Senator Vandenberg called the recommendations a "mere vagrant flirtation" with share-the-wealth ideas.

It was not at all clear, however, as Morgenthau quickly discovered, whether Roosevelt wanted Congress to act at that session or whether he would fight for more than a nominal inheritance tax. The President's intentions were obscured in his puzzling relationship with the cautious Chairman of the Senate Finance Committee, Pat Harrison of Mississippi. Harrison, a masterful parliamentarian who used his considerable power gently but effectively in the cause of fiscal conservatism, opposed the inheritance tax. Roosevelt told him, Morgenthau learned, that the tax should exempt approximately $300,000, which the Secretary considered far too much. Worse still, Morgenthau found it hard to understand the President's shifting tactics.

They changed rapidly during the week after his message. At first Roosevelt stood against having the Senate attach major taxes to the House's resolution extending nuisance taxes—excises on a variety of consumer goods. Harrison, too, apparently with the consent of the White House, spoke out for leaving major reforms to the House, where revenue legislation was supposed to originate. He also advocated postponing the inheritance tax to the following session of Congress. Led by La Follette, however, twenty-two progressive senators agreed to keep Congress in session until it adopted the President's program. Responding to this pressure, Roosevelt and the Democratic congressional leaders announced after a conference of June 25 that they would drive for immediate action. The next day Harrison said the Senate would take the initiative. Yet a day later, the Senate returned to the original schedule, leaving the initiative with the House; Roosevelt told the press he had never intimated that Congress should push through such an important measure; and Harrison, though he was obviously surprised, remained unruffled at this sudden reversal.

These developments gave Morgenthau no indication of just what Roosevelt expected from him. Perhaps the President was not sure himself. He was involved in so many things—among others, antitrust and banking bills, social security, and a bill to

regulate the bituminous coal industry—that he had inadequate
time for studying revenue legislation. Without pressing him, Morgenthau tried to get his signals straight. He did not know, he told
Roosevelt at luncheon on June 26, how to reply to a request from
La Follette for the Treasury's working papers on the inheritance
tax. Roosevelt told him to stall.

"Mr. President," Morgenthau asked, "just strictly between the
two of us, do you or do you not want your Inheritance Tax program passed at this session?"

"Strictly between the two of us," Roosevelt said, "I do not know,
I am on an hourly basis and the situation changes almost mo-
mentarily."

That afternoon Morgenthau told La Follette that there were a
lot of things going on which he did not understand. The Secretary would not give the senator any official recommendations for
taxes, but, he suggested, if La Follette, through Chairman Harrison, requested Treasury experts to bring materials to the Finance Committee, the experts would, of course, comply. This
would give La Follette what he wanted, take Morgenthau out
of a tough spot, and perhaps, as they saw it, keep Harrison from
blocking Roosevelt's "swell message."

While La Follette worked to enlist Senate support for an inheritance tax, Morgenthau on July 8 testified before the House
Ways and Means Committee. Roosevelt had again told him he
would not resist a movement for adjournment before a revenue
act was passed, but he had also said he wanted the Treasury to
stress taxing inheritances as if they were annual personal income,
a method he had earlier asked Morgenthau to "soft-pedal." This
change of heart encouraged the Secretary who in his testimony
emphasized the importance of the revenue that a high inheritance
tax would yield. Although the Treasury felt it unwise to impose
taxes that would retard recovery, he said, it considered it folly
not to tap resources of taxation that would reduce the national
debt without interfering with recovery. He believed that the inheritance tax fell into that category, and he suggested earmark-
ing all revenues from it to lessen future borrowing and ultimately
to pay off the debt.

The Ways and Means Committee included the inheritance tax
in its bill, but the Senate, increasingly resistant, shared the skep-
ticism of the conservative press about Morgenthau's references to

balancing the budget. Roosevelt's hesitation made the Treasury's situation difficult, as did his rejection of one of Harrison's candidates for the Board of Tax Appeals. The senator now favored increasing the rates of the estate tax, which, he argued, would be easier to administer. Morgenthau and his advisers told Roosevelt that a mere increase in those rates would be inconsistent with his message, for it would not apply the principle of the ability to pay. It would take as much from an estate destined for one heir as from one destined for many. The Secretary therefore urged the application of an inheritance tax at least to large bequests.

The Treasury's determination must have impressed the President, whose attention was increasingly available as Congress passed one after another of the Administration's measures. In mid-July he was reported to be agreeable to deferring action, but a few weeks later he permitted Robert Jackson, then Assistant General Counsel of the Treasury, to speak for him as well as for Morgenthau in vigorous testimony before the Senate Finance Committee. Jackson on August 6 rehearsed the Treasury's case, gave priority to the need for revenue, but emphasized the importance of adjusting the tax structure so that it would bear most heavily on those best able to pay. He argued also for using taxes to break up large private fortunes and concentrations of corporate power, to redistribute wealth and equalize business competition. Repeating the recommendations for new taxes which Roosevelt's message had earlier made, Jackson provided the senators with a forceful reminder of the President's purpose. The testimony, Morgenthau recalled years later, was exactly what he had hoped for.

The Revenue Act of 1935, which the Finance Committee drafted, was less satisfactory, but it was nevertheless a landmark in the history of American taxation. Though the committee in the end rejected the inheritance tax, it increased estate taxes markedly and raised individual surtax rates on incomes from 59 per cent at the top to 75 per cent. As the Treasury and the President had recommended, it imposed both a graduated corporate income tax and a tax on intercorporate dividends. The Act assured the Treasury of new revenues; less than Morgenthau had wanted but more than a less aggressive Secretary could have obtained. To his gratification, moreover, in spite of its limitations, the Act advanced the principles he and Roosevelt had advocated.

The Secretary had pursued his objectives steadily since reporting to the President in December 1934. Even if Roosevelt had joined the fight earlier, the conservatives in the Senate might not have yielded more than they did. As it was, the Treasury could measure its success by the dismay of most wealthy Americans. Roy Howard, for one, originally a supporter of Roosevelt, now wrote that businessmen were "frightened," convinced that the new law "aimed at revenge rather than revenue." This interpretation characterized the hostile thinking of those in high income brackets, whose opposition to the New Deal grew as the Treasury pressed for the adoption of significant parts of its program which the Revenue Act of 1935 omitted.

Taxation and Monopoly Power

Fritz Machlup is Walker Professor of Economics at Princeton University. This article is taken from his The Political Economy of Monopoly, *published in 1952.*

IF THE POWER to tax is the power to destroy, taxation, one might think, could have been used for the destruction of monopoly. Perhaps such use would have been undesirable; perhaps it would have been impossible; but one thing is certain: it has not been tried.

NON-FISCAL VERSUS FISCAL OBJECTIVES

The use of taxation for other than strictly fiscal purposes has often been attacked as an unwise exercise of governmental power. There are so many things that society wishes to do, so many objectives to achieve. If taxes were devised on a grand scale as deterrents and incentives, meting out penalties for socially undesirable behavior and giving indirect premiums for socially desirable behavior, the danger would be great that the tax system could not fulfill its primary functions, to raise revenue for the government and avoid inflation. The tax structure might be undermined by gradual accretions of non-fiscal taxes serving many different social purposes.

The purist in public finance who rejects any and all non-fiscal functions of taxation on the ground that they might interfere with the fiscal one apparently has a very narrow view of the governmental agenda. No doubt, he is correct in warning of the social costs that may arise from the damage to a tax system burdened with non-fiscal functions. But he forgets to compare these costs with the costs of attempting to fulfill the same functions by different methods or of failing to fulfill them at all. If an important social objective cannot be attained by other methods, or if it can be attained only at higher costs, one should not let the fact that the tax system might suffer damage as a revenue-raising machine be the overriding consideration. The relative importance of the social objectives, the relative merits and demerits of achieving them in alternative ways, as well as the effects on the tax structure must all be carefully evaluated.

Any tax system has non-fiscal implications. Although taxes may be imposed primarily to raise revenue or as part of an overall fiscal policy, they will always affect such things as the distribution of income, economic incentives, and the availability of capital. Their burden may lie with unequal weight on different size firms or on different types of expansion and thus they incidentally become relevant to the question of monopoly and competition. If the prevention of monopolistic domination of the eeconomy is one of the established policies of government, it is not permissible to neglect the actual effects of the tax system as it is as well as the potential effects of the tax system as it might be.

CORPORATION INCOME TAXES: WHY AND HOW?

For the most part taxation has little relevance for the problem of monopolistic business practices nor can it be easily used to control monopoly as such. Proposals for a direct tax on "monopoly profits" have been made. It is difficult enough to identify profits; to separate monopoly profits from other elements in the net income of a business is impossible. Income taxation can touch monopoly only to the extent that *size* is closely associated with monopoly power. It would be technically possible to tax large corporations out of existence. Or through imposing steeply progressive taxes upon corporations it would be possible to discourage firms from growing larger and to encourage large firms to split up.

All this presupposes that we have and retain corporation taxes at all. Whether they are economically sound and "desirable" is a highly controversial issue. Many economists maintain that business taxes of any kind—sales and excise taxes, excess profits taxes, corporate income taxes, etc.,—are fundamentally unsound because they influence production policies, pricing policies, investment policies of businessmen, which should be determined exclusively by the demand of consumers and the conditions of production. An excise tax may cause producers to produce less than they would otherwise decide to produce. An excess profits tax discourages efforts to reduce costs, promotes wasteful expen-

ditures and may even cause firms to pay higher prices for productive factors than they would pay in the absence of the tax.
A corporation income tax may influence investment decisions of
the firm by creating a bias against the more risky investments. In
order to avoid all such effects, it is forcefully argued, taxes should
not be imposed on business firms but only directly on individuals.

Since individuals must, in the last analysis, bear the taxes anyway, it is also argued on grounds of equity that all taxes be placed
directly and openly on the individuals who bear them. Taxes cannot be "borne" by "artificial" persons, i.e., corporations, but always fall on the real individuals who have an interest in the
corporation's activities as producers, consumers, or suppliers of
capital. Hence an income tax on corporations is ultimately imposed on individuals in a concealed fashion without reference to
any principles of equity or ability to pay. There is, therefore, a
strong case for placing the taxes directly on individuals in accordance with accepted principles of taxation rather than on the
earnings of corporations. Administratively this would be more difficult than the present system, the change would result in considerable upheaval and the squawks of the taxpayers would be
intensified. The chief advantage of the corporation income tax is
that its incidence is concealed from those who bear it and they
can therefore be plucked without excessive pother—surely a
somewhat specious principle of taxation!

These are objections to the principle of corporation taxes. Objections can also be made to the particular way in which they are
constructed. In the United States, for example, many economists
strongly object to the "double taxation of dividends" which results from the fact that the net income of corporations is fully
taxed before dividends are distributed and that the dividends
are taxed again under the personal income tax when the shareholders receive them. The double taxation discriminates against
equity financing and in favor of debt financing, because interest
payments, deductible from taxable corporate income, are taxed
only once. This discrimination may have harmful economic effects,
particularly in downswings of the business cycle, when debt may
become dangerously burdensome.

Nonetheless, we have had corporation taxes for a long time and
we are likely to have them for a long time in the future. Let
us, then, take their existence for granted and examine their rela-

tion to an antimonopoly program. Except for a slight graduation in the corporation income tax rates, the accepted policy has been to make taxes "neutral" with respect to large versus small business. Should taxes perhaps be so devised that they discriminate against big business? Have they perhaps, as many say, been so devised that they have in fact discriminated against small business?

THE ACTUAL BIAS AGAINST SMALL BUSINESS

In one sense it may be said that any business tax whatever—unless it is prohibitively progressive—falls harder on small business than on big. Small businesses depend for their development almost entirely on the reinvestment of their earnings. They do not have the access to the credit and capital markets that large corporations have. Thus a tax on the earnings of business, large or small, reduces the only important source of funds available to small business.

To prevent the tax system from aggravating the difficulty small business faces in raising capital, numerous proposals have been made for completely or partially exempting small firms from the corporation income tax, for a more graduated corporation income tax, for the modification of the special surtax that is levied on profits retained in excess of "reasonable" business needs, for accelerated depreciation allowances for durable assets, and for measures to place incorporated and non-incorporated small business on a more nearly equal basis. This is not the place to discuss these measures. Each of them raises special problems, administrative as well as economic, with regard to efficiency as well as equity.

One particular way in which business income taxes have discriminated against new and small firms concerns the incidence of losses. When large diversified established firms enter new lines of activity, losses made in these lines may be offset for tax purposes against profits made in other lines, so that the taxable income of the firm is reduced by the amount of the losses. Such savings on income tax liability do not exist for the small, new firm, because it has no other departments making profits part of which could become non-taxable on account of the loss offset. The small, new firm is therefore at a distinct disadvantage in any risky enterprise.

This disadvantage is aggravated if income taxes are figured on a strictly annual basis so that losses made in one year cannot be offset against gains in other years. The risk of investing in small firms is thus greater than in large firms and investment in them is discouraged. To remove this bias against small firms the law now provides that net losses in the current year may for tax purposes be "carried back" and set off against income in the two preceding years, and any loss balance still remaining may be "carried forward" against income in the two following years. The carry-back provisions may be very important for small businesses, especially in times of depression when their cash position is likely to be weak; they may then find considerable relief in receiving from the Treasury the cash refunds from taxes paid in the previous two years. But the carry-back provisions are of no help to a *new* firm established for a new venture. Nor will the carry-forward provisions help such a firm if the losses made force it out of business. Thus the new, small firm has neither profits from other departments, nor profits from past years, nor perhaps profits in future years, against which to offset its losses. While, through such loss offsets and consequent tax reductions, the Government shares in the venture losses of old or large firms, it does not do so in the venture losses of new small firms.

If an increase in the concentration of industry in the hands of large business firms is to be prevented (and a decrease in concentration to be promoted) a high birth and survival rate of new firms and high growth rates of small firms are needed. Yet both are cut down by high income taxes. High personal income taxes reduce the capacity of individuals to accumulate funds needed to start new businesses and to nurse them through their formative stages. High corporate income taxes reduce the capacity of the new and small businesses to retain earnings to finance their development and growth, and reduce also the willingness of outsiders to furnish capital for the growth of small firms. In all these respects the small firm is severely handicapped relative to the old and established firm.

In at least one industry the existence of *specific excise taxes* has worked to the disadvantage of small producers and in favor of the dominating concerns. Cigarette taxes, levied by the Federal Government as well as by the states, clearly discourage price competition inasmuch as they reduce the responsiveness of demand to price changes by cigarette manufacturers and as they fall, because they are based on quantity rather than value, relatively more heavily on the cheaper brands. If the abolition of cigarette taxes is not practicable because of fiscal necessity or convenience, they could at least be changed to graduated or *ad valorem* taxes in order to eliminate the present bias against the producers of cheaper products.

TAX-INDUCED SALES OF SMALL BUSINESS FIRMS

Apart from the inherent general bias of the income tax system against small business, a combination of other features in the existing tax system has operated to encourage merger of small businesses with large. The small corporation is frequently closely held, that is, the ownership is confined to a few men, and the equity in it very often accounts for a large proportion of the owners' assets. On the death of an owner, a tax which must be paid in cash is levied on his estate. In order to accumulate enough cash to meet the estate tax an owner, or his heirs, may have to sell his equity in the business. But there is virtually no market for the stock of small corporations, except among large corporations in the same or connected fields which frequently are willing to absorb their smaller competitors. The estate tax, therefore, puts pressure upon owners of small companies to sell out to the big concerns. Alternatively, instead of a cash sale, an owner may prefer to arrange for an exchange of the stock of his firm for the much more saleable stock of the large corporation.

An owner could, of course, prepare for the payment of death duties by distributing to himself in the form of dividends more or all of the profits of his small corporation. But, apart from his desire to leave in the firm as much of his earnings as he can possibly spare, the dividends would be subject to personal income taxation, and he would be loath to pay these taxes on dividends which he takes only in order to prepare for the payment of the estate taxes. Moreover, this way of taking the profits of a corporation is much more expensive than the alternative of realizing a capital gain— which is taxed at a lower rate than dividend income. In other words, the difference between capital gains tax and ordinary income tax militates against dividend distribution and for the retention of the corporate earnings in the company and the eventual realization of the profit through the sale of the appreciated shares of stock. Hence, "the impact of the estate tax on the owners of closely held companies is reinforced by the combined effects of high income taxes and of low capital gains tax rates."

The possibility of a tax advantage is business profits are taken in the form of capital gains rather than dividends may also encourage the owner of a growing but still risky business to cash in his gain at the low rate by selling out and investing in some less risky securities. In other words, he leaves the profits in the business, allowing it to grow and allowing himself to save some personal income tax, then he sells out to a large corporation and takes his profit at the lower tax rate. There is no easy answer to this problem; it would be very wrong to assume that it could or should be solved by eliminating the special treatment of capital gains; indeed, many other serious difficulties would arise if this were done. But the fact remains that the existing system works for the absorption of small business firms by big business firms and thus, indirectly, probably for the reduction of competition and the increase in monopoly power.

THE POTENTIAL BIAS AGAINST BIG BUSINESS

While it may be desirable to reduce as far as possible the weight of taxes on small struggling businesses, it is chimerical to think that this in itself is going to have much effect on monopoly, given the present size of the large units. A tenderness for small business can easily become a blinder preventing adequate attention being given to the continuing growth of large monopolistic business. Although the idea of special taxation of large corporate units suggests itself readily to antagonists of big business, it has never been an accepted principle of tax policy to any significant extent.

A *steeply progressive income tax* has been one of the more popular proposals for reaching large corporations, but has not been adopted in the United States. The 1950 law has only two brackets: a flat normal tax of 25 per cent on all income and an additional tax (surtax) of 22 per cent on all income above $25,000, so that on all income in excess of $25,000 a corporation pays a tax of 47 per cent. A really progressive income tax would have many more brackets, beginning with low rates on the lower incomes and rising steeply as income increased. The effect of such a tax would be to increase the relative profitability of small businesses as compared to large businesses. It might provide a positive incentive for large corporations to break up into independent units, and it might cause businessmen to refrain from expanding their firms to the point where they get into really high income brackets.

Undoubtedly, there would be ways of evading a progressive tax; indeed some broad avenues of evasion are obvious even to the non-expert. The taxable income of corporations is an accounting figure and a stiff tax would intensify pressures to reduce this figure, for example, by resorting to debt financing instead of equity financing (since interest payments are deductible from net income for tax purposes while dividends are paid out of taxable earnings). Similarly the earnings of one corporation might be siphoned into other corporations by means of royalty payments under patent license contracts, fees under management contracts, and similar payments deductible as "expenses" on the part of the corporation paying them. "Split ups" of large corporations into smaller corporations with control remaining in a parent company would probably be attempted. But some methods of preventing this type of evasion are also quite obvious. For example, all dividends received by one corporation from other corporations might be fully taxed, so that the income received by a parent corporation from its subsidiaries would be doubly taxed (first as income of the subsidiary and second as dividend income to the parent corporation). As a matter of fact, all dividend income was fully taxed under the Revenue Acts of 1913 and 1916. This was explained on the grounds that

we did not want holding companies to be encouraged by the tax laws of the country. Upon the contrary, we did desire to discourage them. We also desired to discourage the system of interlocking stockholders, which has led to very much abuse.

This desire to use tax measures to discourage holding companies could not stand up against the pleas of large business that they were being doubly taxed, and similar complaints from small firms with dividend income and from insurance companies and investment concerns who merely helped small stockholders diversify their risks. The law was changed, and from 1917 to 1935 intercorporate dividend income was free from taxation. In 1935, however, President Roosevelt recommended to Congress that intercorporate dividends be taxed in order to prevent evasion of the graduated income tax he proposed. Since 1935, intercorporate dividends have been taxed, but at a rate equivalent to only

15 per cent of the rate on other corporate income. Compared to the alternative of full taxation of dividend income this is only a sop to those desiring to discourage the creation of holding companies.

If intercorporate dividends were fully taxed and the income tax rates were steeply progressive, the question whether an affiliated group of corporations should be allowed to present a consolidated income statement for tax purposes would become much less important than it is at present. When a group of corporations presents a consolidated income statement, it enables them to offset losses of one corporation against gains of others, so that the net income of the group is reduced by the amount of the losses, and furthermore it enables them to avoid the tax on intercorporate dividends. On the other hand, the aggregate taxable income of the group is increased—and, under a progressive scheme, would be in a much higher tax bracket.

If the tax rates are not progressive, a clear tax gain is frequently obtained by presenting a consolidated statement. At present an additional tax of 2 per cent is imposed on the surtax net income of a group of corporations presenting a consolidated income statement. This is supposed to offset the advantages offered to large groups by the consolidated return. But since corporations would not in general use consolidated returns unless there were advantages in so doing, it has been suggested that such returns should either be prohibited (in which case all firms in an affiliated group would be fully taxed as separate entities) or be made compulsory (in order that the group as a unit could not escape taxation in higher income brackets). Clearly, however, if intercorporate dividends were fully taxed and tax rates were progressive, there would not be very much gained one way or the other.

All questions of administrative feasibility, possibilities of evasion, and possibilities of prevention of evasion are, however, far less significant than the question whether a steeply progressive corporation income tax is really a sensible method of controlling the size of corporations. To the extent that the amount of profit and the size of the business unit are correlated, such a tax would get at bigness, and to the extent that bigness and monopoly power are correlated, it would get at monopoly power. But we know that these correlations are far from perfect. They fail chiefly because the efficient size of the business unit is different in different industries. While it may be most desirable that taxes discourage size

that is far in excess of technological or organizational requirements, it is not at all desirable that it discourage or penalize size
that is necessary for efficient operations. It may be absolutely unnecessary, for example, for a flour mill to earn x million dollars a
year, for this might indicate that the firm is far bigger than it has
to be in order to operate efficiently. But the same x million dollars
may be an impossibly small profit for a manufacturer of automo-
biles, who has to be big in order to be efficient.

In other words, large and small are relative terms. A large ant
is appreciably smaller than a small dog. And so it is with firms.
The Department of Commerce sets standards of what is to be considered large or small differently for retail and for wholesale firms.
The Federal Trade Commission has gone further and set up different definitions of small companies according to whether the
company is in the field of cement manufacturing, steel, petroleum,
sugar, etc. A large firm, from our point of view, is a firm in a position to dominate or exercise appreciable influence over an entire
industry, but the size of the firm in a position to do this in one
industry may have no relation to the size of firms in similar positions in other industries. Hence, a graduated corporation income
tax intended to discourage the growth of firms beyond the technically most efficient size, but imposing the same rates on all firms
with the same income even though they belong to industries as
diverse as retail trade and public utilities, would penalize some
firms for being as big as they must be to exist at all, while permitting others to grow big enough to dominate their industries.

A steeply progressive tax would force firms to weigh the tax
savings if they remained (or became) small, and therefore in the
lower tax brackets, against the profitability of growing (or remaining) large. But since the profitability of growing (or being) larger
includes not only the economies of large-scale production but also
the monopoly profits from a greater control of the market, any tax
system which deterred firms from striving for monopoly would
also deter them from taking full advantage of the technical economies of large scale.

It might be a way out of this dilemma to adopt different income
brackets for different industries or at least grant relief from the
"prohibitive" tax rates of the high brackets to those industries
where firms must needs be big and their earnings correspondingly
large. But in any event it is understandable why opponents of

monopoly have hesitated to propose radical progression in the rate schedule of the corporate income tax.

DIFFERENTIAL TAXES ON RETAINED EARNINGS

Since a large part of the growth of business firms is financed out of retained earnings and since the present system of corporate income taxation restricts the internal financing of growth of small companies much more severely than that of large ones, differential taxation of undistributed profits might be used to offset the present handicap.

Of course, the present obstacles to the growth of small firms should not be made worse and, hence, no additional taxes should be levied on the undistributed profits of corporations below a certain size, or on undistributed profits below certain amounts. But a strong case can be made for a graduated tax on retained earnings to check the sustained growth of very large corporations. These corporate giants with their easy access to the capital market do not have to rely on internal financing if they should need additional funds for profitable expansion. There is no reason why they should not distribute more of their earnings and then raise on the market the capital they need to carry out promising investment projects.

Differential taxation of undistributed profits—with generous exemptions, leaving small business firms without additional tax burdens, but cutting deeply into the retained earnings of the largest corporations—would not merely equalize the effects of taxation on the financing of business growth, but might incidentally serve also as incentive for corporate split-ups. Needless to say, one would have to ensure that these split-ups of corporate concerns desiring to avoid the tax are *bona fide* and effective dissolutions and not merely sham separations to evade the tax obligation.

TAX POLICY AND ANTIMONOPOLY POLICY

Steep progression in the corporate income tax, heavier taxation of intercorporate dividends, and graduated taxes on very large undistributed profits are not the only tax measures proposed as weapons against bigness and concentration. Other possibilities have been suggested, for example, graduated sales taxes,

taxes on the number of establishments, taxes according to the number of employees. But very little thought has been given to the whole subject of using tax policies to combat concentration.

A suggestion which is directed more against monopolistic practices than against bigness or concentration concerns the eligibility of corporate expenses as deductions from taxable income. Expenses whose chief function is to enable the corporation to improve or maintain a monopolistic position might be made nondeductible for income tax purposes, for example, advertising expenses in excess of a certain percentage of sales, or excessive expenditures for certain kinds of litigation.

In certain fields, such as the cigarette industry, where advertising is "the key to the monopoly problem," taxation of advertising "would appear to offer a promising . . . line of attack." Since the main objective of such a tax would be to reduce the handicap of small or new firms as against large national advertisers, the tax would have to be graduated, leaving smaller amounts of advertising outlays tax-free while levying progressively increasing rates on larger outlays. But the use of a single set of tax brackets (in terms of dollars spent for advertising) for all industries would not be advisable in view of the wide differences in organization, products and market. On the other hand, the proposal of a tax schedule in terms of the "percentage of selling expenses to total expenses" overlooks the fact that new firms entering an industry and small firms attempting to grow larger may have to spend a larger percentage on advertising than firmly established companies. Hence, "it is proposed that tax brackets [for the advertising tax] be determined upon the basis of market control, rates varying according to the individual firm's percentage of national sales of each general class of product."

Most tax lawyers are horrified at the suggestion that the tax system be "misused" to combat monopoly, just as most corporation lawyers are horrified at the analogous suggestion with regard to the corporation laws. Everybody professes to be wholehearted for a campaign against monopoly, but protests against fighting it in his own field of competence. The idea of using tax policy as an aid to antimonopoly policy is attractive in that it may reverse the direction in which the profit motive usually works by making it more profitable to become smaller. The incentive method has often great advantages over the prohibition method.

Suggested Further Readings

This brief bibliography, organized according to the major divisions of this volume, is designed for the reader who wants to extend his study of public policies and their politics. Specific articles in periodicals such as *Fortune*, *Reporter*, and *Science* are not listed but it should be noted that they are excellent sources for someone interested in techniques of government control or in policies and politics generally. The items listed under general reading should prove particularly useful in examining the ties between techniques and other economic and political considerations.

GENERAL READING

Benedict, Murray R., *Farm Policies of the United States, 1790–1950* (Twentieth Century Fund, 1953). Makes clear the multiple techniques that can be used in a single field.

Commission on Money and Credit, *Money and Credit* (Prentice-Hall, 1961). Chapter 9, "The Choice and Combination of Policy Instruments," suggests the complexities involved in mixing and matching techniques to gain specific ends.

Fainsod, Merle, Lincoln Gordon, and Joseph C. Palamountain, Jr., *Government and the American Economy* (Norton, 1959, 3rd ed.).

Palamountain, Joseph C., Jr., *The Politics of Distribution* (Harvard University Press, 1955).

Temporary National Economic Committee, *Investigation of Concentration of Economic Power*, monographs nos. 19, 20, and 21 (Government Printing Office, 1940).

SUBSIDY

Dupre, J. Stefan and W. Eric Gustafson, "Contracting for Defense," *Political Science Quarterly* (June 1962). Illustrates how an ostensibly private group of contractors can actually use the technique of contracting to make governmental policy.

Foss, Philip O., *Politics and Grass* (University of Washington, 1960). A classic case of regulation becoming subsidy through the activities of the most powerful of the regulated.

Gilpatrick, Thomas V., "Price Support Policy and the Midwest Farm Vote," *Midwest Journal of Political Science* (November 1959).

Hardin, Charles M., "Reflections on Agricultural Policy Formulation in the United States," *American Political Science Review* (October 1948).

Hardin, Charles M., "Political Influence and Agricultural Research," *American Political Science Review* (August 1947).

Hathaway, Dale E. and Lawrence E. Witt, "Agricultural Policy: Whose Valuations?", *Journal of Farm Economics* (August 1952).

Johnson, D. Gale, "Agricultural Credit, Capital, and Credit Policy in the United States," in Commission on Money and Credit, *Federal Credit Programs* (Prentice-Hall, 1963).

"Management of Public Land Resources," *Yale Law Journal* (March 1951).

Miller, J. P., "The Pricing Effects of Accelerated Amortization," *Review of Economics and Statistics* (February 1952).

Morgan, Robert J., "Pressure Politics and Resources Administration," *Journal of Politics* (February 1956).

Pennock, J. Roland, "Party and Constituency in Postwar Agricultural Price-Support Legislation," *Journal of Politics* (May 1956).

Ripley, Randall B., "Bargaining in the House: The Food Stamp Act of 1964" and "Congress Considers Federal Aid to Airports, 1958–59" in Frederic N. Cleaveland, ed., *Congress and Urban Problems* (The Brookings Institution, 1966).

Surrey, Stanley S., "The Congress and the Tax Lobbyist: How Special Tax Provisions Get Enacted," *Harvard Law Review* (May 1957).

REGULATION

Bernstein, Marver, *Regulating Business by Independent Commission* (Princeton University Press, 1955).

Fainsod, Merle, "Some Reflections on the Nature of the Regulatory Process," in *Public Policy* (Harvard University Press, 1940), volume 1.

Huntington, Samuel P., "The Marasmus of the ICC: The Commission, the Railroads, and the Public Interest," *Yale Law Journal* (April 1952).

Jennings, M. Kent, "Politics and Pollution: Congressional Action in Water Pollution Control," in Frederic N. Cleaveland, ed., *Congress and Urban Problems* (Brookings, 1966).

Jennings, Richard W., "Self-Regulation in the Securities Industry: The Role of the Securities Exchange Commission," *Law and Contemporary Problems,* (Summer 1964).

Landis, James M., "Legislative History of the Securities Act of 1933," *George Washington Law Review* (October 1959).

Quesada, E. R., "The Pressures Against Air Safety," *Harper's* (January 1961).

Ripley, Randall B., "'Congress Supports Clean Air, 1963," in Frederic N. Cleaveland (ed.), *Congress and Urban Problems* (Brookings, 1966).

Rosenblum, Victor G., "How to Get into TV: The Federal Communications Commission and Miami's Channel 10," in Alan F. Westin, ed., *The Uses of Power* (Harcourt, Brace & World, 1962).

Whitney, Simon N., *Antitrust Policies: American Experience in Twenty Industries* (Twentieth Century Fund, 1958).

MANIPULATION

Adams, Walter and Horace M. Gray, *Monopoly in America* (Macmillan, 1955). See particularly Chapter 4, which discusses specific tax techniques which promote monopoly.

Blough, Roy, *The Federal Taxing Policy* (Prentice-Hall, 1952).

Burns, Eveline, *The American Social Security System* (Houghton Mifflin, 1949).

Committee on Economic Security, *Report to the President* (Government Printing Office, 1935).

Douglas, Paul H., *Social Security in the United States* (McGraw-Hill, 1936).

Forsythe, John S., "Legislative History of the Fair Labor Standards Act," *Law and Contemporary Problems* (Summer 1939). This indicates how exemptions can be the price for giving the government a new technique to use for manipulative ends.

President's Committee on Civil Rights, *To Secure These Rights* (Government Printing Office, 1947).

Smithies, Arthur, "Uses of Selective Credit Controls," in *United States Monetary Policy* (The American Assembly, 1958).

Problems of Modern Government

General Editor: THEODORE J. LOWI, *University of Chicago*

This new Norton series of paperbound volumes is planned to provide intensive study of the outstanding questions of public policy. In each volume specific policy issues are viewed within their political context, enabling the reader to grasp the basic techniques of governmental control. It is through a clear understanding of policies and their relevance to political institutions, processes, and behavior that the student comes to understand the nature of modern government. The policy approach can be utilized in many courses, though it has particular value in adding a lively new dimension to the introductory American government course.

Public Policies and Their Politics: An Introduction to the Techniques of Government Control
Edited by Randall B. Ripley

In preparation

Equality
Edited by John H. Schaar

The Politics of Education
Edited by George La Noue

Private Life and Public Order
Edited by Theodore J. Lowi

THE EDITOR

Randall B. Ripley is Research Associate in Governmental Studies at the Brookings Institution in Washington, D. C. He holds a B.A. from DePauw University and M.A. and Ph.D. from Harvard where his dissertation won the Sumner Prize. He has had articles in the *American Political Science Review* and other leading academic journals.

W · W · NORTON & COMPANY · INC ·
55 Fifth Avenue   New York, N.Y. 10003

254